CELEBRATE THE BIBLE

by

Wanda Pelfrey

illustrated by Kathy Hyndman

Music by:
Frances Mann Benson, Helen Kitchell Evans, Helen Friesen, Muriel Larson, Beulahmae Marchbanks and Phyllis Michael

Cover by Dan Grossmann

Shining Star Publications, Copyright © 1988
A Division of Good Apple, Inc.

ISBN No. 0-86653-453-9

Standardized Subject Code TA ac

Printing No. 9876

Shining Star Publications
A Division of Good Apple, Inc.
Box 299
Carthage, IL 62321-0299

The purchase of this book entitles the buyer to reproduce student activity pages for classroom use only. Any other use requires written permission from Shining Star Publications.

All rights reserved. Printed in the United States of America.

Unless otherwise indicated, the King James Version of the Bible was used in preparing the activities in this book.

DEDICATION

To those whose willing sacrifices allowed me to accept this opportunity God provided for me . . . .

DANNY   KELLIE   SANDY

Shining Star Publications, Copyright © 1988, A division of Good Apple, Inc.

SS847

TABLE OF CONTENTS

The Bible Teaches Us About Creation 5
The Bible Teaches Us About the Ten Commandments 17
The Bible Teaches Us About Kings 29
The Bible Teaches Us How to Praise God 41
The Bible Teaches Us How to Be Wise 53
The Bible Teaches Us How to Listen 65
The Bible Teaches Us How to Follow 77
The Bible Teaches Us How to Be Happy 89
The Bible Teaches Us How to Pray 101
The Bible Teaches About People Like Us 113
Bible Fact Games 125
Answer Key 143
Award Certificates 144

SONGS

The Ten Commandments 25, 26
Youthful David 31
Clap and Praise 47
In the Bible 61
Jonah 68
Stop! Look! And Listen! 76
The Beatitudes 90
The Lord's Prayer 104
Old Testament Books 127
New Testament Books 128

A WORD TO PARENTS & TEACHERS

Any celebration requires at least two elements, something to celebrate and someone with whom to celebrate. This book was created to insure a successful celebration of the Book, the Bible, with children ages 6-11.

To celebrate, we need two kinds of knowledge: knowledge of the children with whom we are working and knowledge of the material being covered. Knowing each child as a person begins with a genuine interest in the child, and as we spend time with him/her that knowledge grows. Bible knowledge is also something that grows. If knowing everything about the Bible was a prerequisite, everyone would be excluded from teaching it. Being in a continual mode of study and growth should include us all. We must constantly ask ourselves two key questions: (1) Do I know my class members better this week than I did last week? (2) Do I know my Bible better this week than I did last week?

Some people are born cheerleaders, while many are not. All of us, however, possess a certain degree of enthusiasm for the things we love. Do we eagerly prepare for and look forward to the times we spend with our children? If not, we should make it a matter of prayer and reflection. Perhaps we do not know the children well enough. Children do not want or need our dutiful presence. They do, however, want and require our joyful participation in their lives. If we are knowledgeable and enthusiastic when working with children, they will catch that enthusiasm and learn to celebrate Bible-based learning.

Let us, parents and teachers, lead a celebration of the Bible, and pray that it will be the beginning of a lifelong celebration for the children we teach.

THE BIBLE TEACHES US ABOUT CREATION

It is difficult for all of us to realize the scope of the creation. It is even more difficult for young children. Share the story of the creation, presented in Genesis, and use the activities that follow to help you teach the difficult to understand subject, CREATION, to your youngsters.

Bulletin Board Idea

PURPOSE: To give children a visual image of the order of creation.

PROCEDURE:
1. Use an overhead projector to enlarge the numerals 1-7 in the picture above on different colored poster board.
2. Cut out each numeral.
3. Mount pictures from old magazines to illustrate the days of creation to each numeral. Example: The numeral 4 will have pictures of sun, moon and stars attached to it.
4. Cover the bulletin board with light blue paper.
5. Attach the numerals to the bulletin boards.

ADDITIONAL ACTIVITY: Let each child cut out construction paper numerals 1-7 and illustrate his own numerals to take home.

Shining Star Publications, Copyright © 1988, A division of Good Apple, Inc.

SS847

LIGHT AND DARKNESS LEARNING ACTIVITIES

"This is the day which the Lord hath made . . . ." Psalm 118:24

TOTAL DARKNESS

Find an area without an outside source of light. Ask the children if they have ever been in total darkness. Warn them that you are going to turn off the lights. (If you have very young children in the room, have them hold hands. Be sensitive to the fact that one or two might prefer not to participate and plan ahead.) Ask the children to think about certain things when the lights are off.

1. What they hear.
2. Does the room feel bigger or smaller?
3. What does total darkness look like?

Quote Genesis 1:1-2. Do not leave the lights off for more than 30 seconds. If someone becomes frightened, turn them on immediately.

Turn on the light and quote Genesis 1:3. Ask the children to talk about the difference light makes.

LIGHT . . . .

Provide several simple reference books from your public library. Help the children find out how light makes a difference in:

1. plants
2. people
3. animals
4. weather

Teach the children what a great gift God gave us when He gave us light.

THE SOURCE OF LIGHT

Display several sources of light such as an electric lamp, a candle, a flashlight and an oil lamp. (If the candle and oil lamp are lit, be sure they are well supervised.)

Ask the children to discuss what they notice about the source of light. They will probably mention the brightness giving off heat, etc. Ask them what the source of all light is? Lead them to realize that God is the source of all light.

GLOW IN THE DARK

Collect as many different "glow in the dark" items as you can find for a display. After exposing them to light, turn off the room lights and let the children look at them. Find simple books to explain how this happens. Remind the children that even though the items glow in the dark, they get their light from another source.

Purchase fluorescent crayons for the children to use in making posters about light and darkness.

EARTH, SKY AND SEA PROJECTS

You can accomplish a lot of teaching while children are up to their elbows in a project. Guiding them in the creation of a terrarium, relief map or papier-mache globe will be rewarding for you and educational for them. As they work, help them compare their great efforts and simple results to the magnificent creation of the universe by God.

TERRARIUM

Obtain a container. An old aquarium or large glass jar (ask at restaurants or school cafeteria) works equally well. Provide sand, potting soil, small plants, shells, rocks, etc. Talk about the need for proper drainage as you put in the sand layer. Lead the children to discuss the many types of plants that grow in different environments (deserts, marshes, mountains, etc.) Point out that God designed the perfect plants for different growing conditions. Keep watch on your terrarium for several weeks to see which plants are best suited to its environment.

COLOR THE EARTH

Use newsprint or table paper to draw a map of the continents and oceans. Try to keep it in reasonable perspective, but don't worry about a lack of great artistic ability. Let the children color the water areas blue and the land areas green or brown. As the children work, read Genesis 1:6-10. Encourage discussion on how they think the world looked during the creation period. Let their imaginations explore many possibilities.

The mind of a child may come closer to fact than the speculations of many scholars. Say, "we are only using two or three colors on our map. How many colors did God use in creating the world?" Seek to help them discover God's power and knowledge.

PAPIER-MÂCHÉ GLOBE

For each globe you wish to make, you will need one round balloon (invest in good quality ones), strips of newspaper and papier-mâché paste.

To make papier-mâché paste, blend 1¾ cups very hot water and ½ cup flour. (Add 1 tablespoon alum if you will be saving the unused papier-mâché paste.)

Spend the first day covering the inflated balloons with several layers of paste-soaked newspaper strips. Dip strips of newspaper in the paste and wrap around the balloons one at a time. Place papier-mâché globes on newspapers to dry.

When completely dry, help the children pencil in outlines of continents. Have the boys and girls paint their globes in the same manner as the "Color the Earth" project. Some of the older pupils may want to go into more detail.

GROWING THINGS

OUTDOOR GARDENING

If a small plot on the church grounds is available to you, take advantage of it. Even a few square feet can give your class the feeling of participation in the growing cycle. Plant foods they can enjoy using later. A hill of potatoes, a couple of tomato plants, some sunflowers and a few stalks of corn or popcorn will give you teaching materials for a later date. A border of marigolds will discourage some pests and add beauty to the garden. (If a larger plot is provided, and you feel you have the ability to do so, you might let your children plant a sharing garden. Food from it could be shared with the needy.)

As you and the children plan the garden, read Genesis 1:11,12. Have the children name as many things as they can think of that are growing in God's garden.

Let upkeep become a regular part of your routine. A few minutes of weeding or watering before class time will keep interest growing.

If a garden plot is not available, perhaps you can get permission to plant a flower border by a walkway or at the home of a shut-in.

Ask the children why they think God created flowers? How many different types of flowers can they name?

INDOOR GARDENING

Provide individual containers for each child. Styrofoam cups, cut-off plastic bottles or milk cartons (small ones can be obtained from schools) make good flower pots. Before planting, let the children decorate and label containers. Tempera paint, Con-Tact paper, crayons and stickers can be used.

Drainage material such as gravel or sand will be needed as well as good potting soil. Marigold or herb seeds are good plant choices.

Cover your work area with newspapers. Show the children how to place a layer of drainage material in the bottom of the container before they fill it with soil. Explain how extra water will drain away from plant roots. Plastic spoons make good shovels.

If the children are going to care for their plants at home, before transporting put them inside plastic bags to prevent spilling. Remind them that they will have to water their plants. Have them think about ways God cares for His plants.

An indoor garden can be made by installing an inexpensive, plastic window box. If the window ledge in your room is too small, a table or bookcase can be placed beneath the window to hold the box.

Let the children decide what to plant. Many flower seeds will do nicely in an inside box. Radishes often will grow inside if your group decides to grow a vegetable.

Hanging baskets for each window will also provide a nice gardening experience.

Keep a written record of the plants in your room. Read Genesis 1:11,12. Ask the children if they think the flowers that God created were already blooming.

Shining Star Publications, Copyright © 1988, A division of Good Apple, Inc. SS847

FUN TO DO

"Many, O Lord my God, are thy wonderful works which thou hast done . . . ." Psalm 40:5

Crossword:

Down:
1.
3.
4.

Across:
2.
3.

Dot to Dot:

COOKING THE THINGS GOD CREATED

BASIC RULES

Children love to cook. Even mixing salad greens can be a creative experience. Cooking with foods they have grown, or with foods like those they are growing, will be a real treat.

The church (or your own) kitchen will provide the best stage for your cooking experiences. Hot plates in classrooms can prove dangerous. Establish some basic safety rules.

1. No loose clothing worn around the stove. Wear aprons to protect clothing.
2. Pot handles turned away from the front of the stove.
3. No playing around the stove.

Careful supervision will assure a safe, enjoyable activity.

BOILED NEW POTATOES

If you are going to use potatoes your children have grown, let them have the joy of digging them. Follow this with a thorough experience in hand and potato washing. Remind the children that while soil is necessary for growing potatoes, it is not desirable for cooking them. Provide vegetables, and nail brushes.

Place the clean potatoes in cold water, add salt and bring to a slow boil. Let the children take turns checking the potatoes by piercing them with a fork.

As they wait for the potatoes to cook, ask each child (or as a group) to write a prayer of thanks for the simple potato.

Boiled new potatoes are delicious plain or with the addition of butter, salt, pepper, chopped parsley or grated cheese.

CORN ON THE COB

If the children have grown sweet corn, they will enjoy pulling the ears off the stalks, husking them and watching you drop them into boiling, salted water. Be sure they are cool enough to eat before serving. (If you buy corn on the cob, select ears that still have the husks on, so the children can experience removing them.)

Ask them to describe the taste of corn on the cob. Have a display of items made from corn, such as cornmeal, corn flakes or other corn cereals, corn oil, corn syrup, etc. Point out God's wisdom in creating a food that can be used in so many ways. Remind the children that it took a long, long time for people to discover how many ways there were to use the gift of corn.

POPCORN

Shelling popcorn off the cob is a good learning experience, but it will taste just as good if it has been commercially bagged. If a popcorn popper is available, this cooking project can be done in the classroom.

Popcorn is a fun food. Have the children describe the fun things that can be done with popcorn. Give thanks for this fun, and "good for us" food.

MASHED POTATOES

Perhaps the peeling of the potatoes should be done by you, the teacher, but the children can probably slice them into small chunks with dull table knives. Again, cook in salted water bringing to a slow boil.

Ask the children, as they wait, to name all the different ways they have eaten potatoes. (There is even a potato candy.) Guide children to the realization that some of God's simple gifts are the most useful.

Shining Star Publications, Copyright © 1988, A division of Good Apple, Inc.

SS847

COLORING PAGE

"... all men shall fear, and shall declare the work of God ...."   Psalm 64:9

Color all "1's" blue and all "2's" yellow to see what God created to put in the sky.

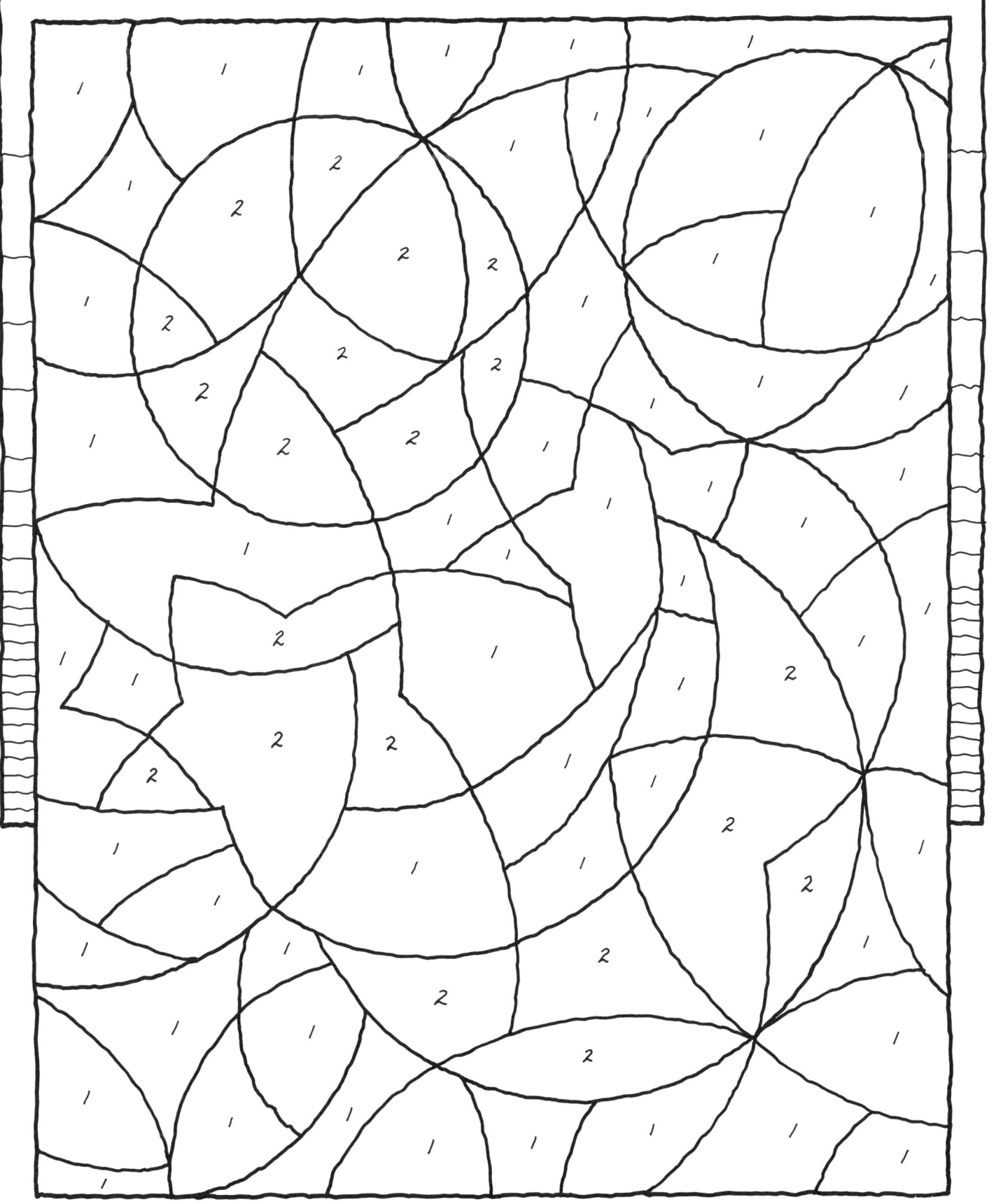

STAR CRAFTS

NEW WORDS

As your children work on their craft projects, let them make up new words to the song, "Twinkle, Twinkle Little Star." Encourage them to sing about God's power and wisdom in creation.

STAR WINDOW HANGING

Give each child an oval of poster board, a star-shaped cookie cutter or pattern and a hat pin. Provide folded towels or other padding to go under the poster board as the children work. Demonstrate how, by carefully punching holes around the pattern, they can put star designs on their poster board. Hold your example in front of a strong lamp or in front of a window, and the light will pass through the holes.

STAR PRINTS

Cut a potato in half. Use a star-shaped cookie cutter to make an imprint on the smooth cut. Carefully trim away the part of the potato surrounding the star imprint. Use the star which is left as a stamp. Ink pads or tempera paint can be used to decorate wrapping paper, napkins, place mats, etc.

GOD-MADE, MAN-MADE

Today we have so many things that are man-made in addition to those that are God-made. Young children have to make those differentiations. Make a set of star-shaped cards with pictures of man-made objects on them and a set with God-made objects on them. Mix them up and let the children sort them into two groups. For more advanced, have them sort the pictures into further groups. For example, for God-made things, sort according to the day they were created.

STAR STENCILS

Use a cookie cutter to trace the pattern of a star onto poster board. An X-acto knife* can be used to carefully cut out the star leaving the stencil whole. Shoe polish daubers transfer paint well. The children can decorate paper, cardboard or wooden items with the stencils. (If your class is large, you will want to make several stencils.)

*An X-acto knife should be used by adults only.

Shining Star Publications, Copyright © 1988, A division of Good Apple, Inc.

SS847

GOD'S SPECIAL CREATION: ME

"... it is he that hath made us, and not we ourselves...." Psalm 100:3

Brainstorm with the children about the things that make people different from animals. Read the account of the creation of Adam and Eve in Genesis 2:4-24. Encourage the children to do one of the following projects.

PRAYER DIARY

Provide small notebooks made from construction paper and notebook paper. Ask the children to write down little prayers to God each day for one or two weeks. (Kindergarten children can draw pictures of things they want to pray about or ask a parent to help them keep a written diary.)

Remind the children that people are the only creation that pray to God.

THIS IS ME COLLAGES

Help children list things that make them unique. Include their favorites: color, food, holiday, etc. Weigh and measure (if it is appropriate) each child so the information can be included on their collages. Next, help the children cut pictures from magazines that depict some of their favorites. Children are to cut and paste pictures, words, photographs, etc. to a large sheet of poster board to create their own collages.

ALL ABOUT PEOPLE

Draw an outline of a person on a large sheet of newsprint. (The children may want to trace around one of their classmates.) Mount this on a wall and let the children fill in as many facts about humans as they can. Ask the children's librarian at your library to help you find some up-to-date, easy reference books. Some facts you might want to include are:
1. How many people are in the world today?
2. How many bones are in the human body?
3. What percentage of the human body is water?
4. How fast do hair and fingernails grow?
5. How many teeth should an adult have?
6. How many different races exist?
7. Items from brainstorming session mentioned above.

Shining Star Publications, Copyright © 1988, A division of Good Apple, Inc.

SS847

HOW THE WORLD BEGAN

Genesis 1,2
by Edith Mize Lewis

This is a read-aloud play. You don't need scenery, costumes or props. Make it come alive. Read it and use your hands (or body) to express your thoughts and how you feel. You may wish to use this action story/poem to introduce the creation activities found on the two following pages. The words of the poem can be used on a creation mural.

CHORUS I:	Once, a long time ago,	(Sadly shake head.)
	There was no world at all—	
	No sun to shine,	(Cross arms over chest.)
	No moonbeams at all.	
CHORUS II:	Then God made the world	
	And water was all around.	(Put finger over lips . . . SSH!)
	Darkness was everywhere	
	And there was no sound.	(Close eyes.)
CHORUS I:	It was an unfriendly place	(Shake head "no.")
	With no day or night.	
	But God looked around and said:	(Look around and say.)
	"Let there be light."	
CHORUS II:	The light became the day.	(Everyone smile.)
	The darkness became the night.	(Everyone frown.)
	The second day He made the sky	(Make a sweeping gesture
	And everything was bright.	with right arm over head.)
CHORUS I:	The third day He made the sea	(Use hands for rolling seas.)
	And then He created dry land.	
	He covered it with a carpet of grass	(Use hands to describe grassy
	With flowers and trees to stand.	land.)
		(Imitate flowers and trees.)
CHORUS II:	The fourth day He made the stars	(Raise hands over head.)
	And the sun and the moon, too.	(Make the sun and the moon.)
	The sun ruled during the day,	(Make a happy face—smile.)
	But at night the moon ruled, too.	(Be very quiet—close eyes.)
CHORUS I:	The fifth day He made living	(Clap hands.)
	Fish to swim and birds to fly.	(Be a fish or a bird.)
	The world became a better place,	
	And above was heaven the sky.	(Sweep right arm over head.)
CHORUS II:	The sixth day He created man	
	And decided to give him a wife.	(Have one boy be Adam and
	He called them Adam and Eve.	one girl will be Eve.)
	And then on earth was life.	
CHORUS I:	The sixth day came to an end.	(Heads down.)
	It was as He had planned.	(Heads up.)
CHORUS II:	The seventh day God rested.	(Close eyes.)
	And then the world began.	(Run around and then sit down.)

CREATION GAME

Reproduce the game pieces found below. Color and cut apart. Attach each game piece to light cardboard and cover with clear Con-Tact paper. Trim around the edges. Now the game is ready to be played.

HOW TO PLAY:

1. Shuffle the cards and place face down in four rows, putting three cards in each row.

2. Each player turns two cards face up. If the two items pictured were created on the same day, the child keeps both pictures and gets to turn two more cards face up.

3. If the two items were not created on the same day, the child turns the cards face down and the next player gets a turn.

4. Game continues until all the cards have been collected.

Shining Star Publications, Copyright © 1988, A division of Good Apple, Inc. SS847

LEARNING ON THE GO

NATURE WALK

Your own church grounds or a nearby park may provide the perfect setting for a visit with God's creation. Take a preview walk and list the things you want the children to see. You may want to mark them in some way. Take along a magnifying glass to study leaves, flowers and small insects.

After looking at each item, give thanks for it and its kind.

STAR WATCHING PARTY

If you live away from city lights and the weather is warm, a star watching party will be a lot of fun.

Use a star theme for decorations and refreshments (See Star Crafts found on page 12.) Star-shaped cookies and sandwiches, Moon pies and Milky Way candy bars will serve well as treats.

Play drop the star in the bucket, pin the moon in the sky, find the stars (played like an Easter egg hunt but using cut out stars), and other star variations of familiar games.

Provide old blankets and sit on the ground outside for a devotional time. Learn the location of some of the star formations. Point them out to the children. Ask them to count the stars. Then they will soon realize that they cannot do so. Help them realize they cannot possibly see all the stars. Read Psalm 147:4. Ask why they think God knows how many stars there are. Lead them in a prayer time of thanksgiving for the beauty of the stars.

VISIT A PLANETARIUM

If you live near a planetarium, why not plan a group trip? Contact an employee of the planetarium about rates, times of shows, etc. before making plans. Send written information about cost, time and type of transportation, home with the children well in advance of the trip. Also send a permission slip. (See reproducible permission slip found on page 28.) Be sure to line up enough adults to supervise the children on the trip.

Meet as a group before entering or before leaving, the planetarium. Read Psalm 148:3. Ask the children to think about God's great power as they watch.

VISIT A ZOO

A nearby zoo also furnishes many examples of God's creative powers.

Again cost, time and transportation need to be checked.

Divide the children into small groups of three to five per adult. Remind these adults to direct the thoughts of the children to the creative power of God as they view the animals.

A picnic, on zoo grounds if possible, will provide a good time for sharing among all the groups. Ask the children to tell what their favorite animals are and why. Ask, "Why do you think God made beavers (goats, rabbits, etc.)?" Give thanks for the many different animals you have seen and for what they mean to our world.

Shining Star Publications, Copyright © 1988, A division of Good Apple, Inc. SS847

THE BIBLE TEACHES US ABOUT THE TEN COMMANDMENTS

Making the Ten Commandments relevant to a child's world is sometimes difficult. The activities and games that follow were designed to help you bring the Ten Commandments to the level of a child's understanding.

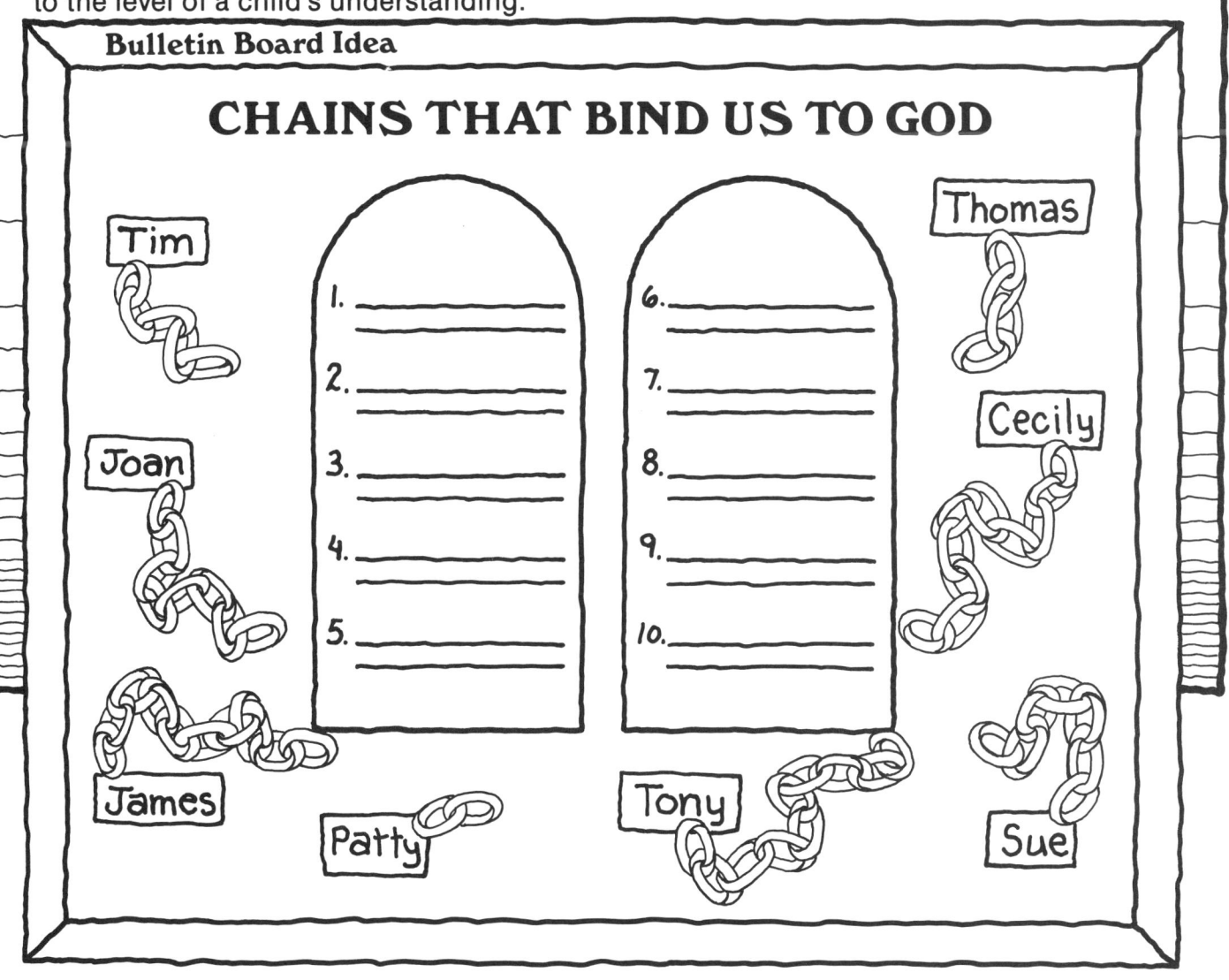

Bulletin Board Idea

CHAINS THAT BIND US TO GOD

Tim · Thomas · Joan · Cecily · James · Patty · Tony · Sue

1. _____
2. _____
3. _____
4. _____
5. _____
6. _____
7. _____
8. _____
9. _____
10. _____

PURPOSE: To familiarize boys and girls with the Ten Commandments. (You will find them in Exodus 20.)

PROCEDURE:
1. Cover the bulletin board with sky blue paper.
2. Use an overhead projector to enlarge the tablets above. Write the Ten Commandments on the tablets and mount on the board. Using a black marker or black cut-out letters, attach the title to the board.
3. Reproduce a copy of the following page for each member of your group. Staple a link, with each child's name, on the bulletin board. Each time a child can recite from memory a commandment, attach the link to that child's chain on the bulletin board. When a child has memorized all Ten Commandments and has a chain with ten links, staple the last link to the edge of the Ten Commandments tablets.

Shining Star Publications, Copyright © 1988, A division of Good Apple, Inc.

SS847

PAPER CHAIN LINKS

1. Thou shalt have no other gods before me.

2. Thou shalt not make unto thee any graven image.

3. Thou shalt not take the name of the Lord thy God in vain.

4. Remember the sabbath day, to keep it holy.

5. Honor thy father and thy mother.

6. Thou shalt not kill.

7. Thou shalt not commit adultery.

8. Thou shalt not steal.

9. Thou shalt not bear false witness against thy neighbour.

10. Thou shalt not covet.

MEMORY GAMES

Children have wonderful minds and usually find memorizing easy; however, sometimes they need to be encouraged when memorizing Scriptures. Helping them to learn methods of memorizing can be a great blessing. Use the four basic formats for memory games found on this page to teach other Bible-based facts.

PUT IT TO MUSIC

Let the children experiment with putting the Ten Commandments to various familiar tunes. Try nursery rhyme tunes, commercial tunes, hymns, etc. The children will be delighted with their "song writing" and will learn the commandments.

GRAB BAG

Number ten index cards 1-10. On the back side of each card write that number's commandment. Let the children take turns drawing a card out of a bag. If they look at the number side first, they are to recite the commandment. If they look at the commandment side first, they are to give the number. Again, this is a learning, not a testing, game.

MATCHUP

On strips of poster board, write the commandments in block letters. Space words so they can be cut between. Cut each in a different way so only correct matches will fit together.

DOUBLE CIRCLE GAME

Draw two large circles on cardboard and divide both into ten sections. In the first number 1 through 10. In the second circle write each commandment in the corresponding space.

Attach a spinner arrow to the first circle and a circle of poster board to the second from which one section has been removed. Have each child spin the arrow and give the appropriate commandment. Children may check by turning the section to the appropriate spot on wheel. This can be used as a large group activity or by small groups or individuals. Remind the children that this is an activity to help them learn, not to test them.

Shining Star Publications, Copyright © 1988, A division of Good Apple, Inc.   SS847

THE LAWS ABOUT GOD

Today's children are often exposed to irreverence. They hear God's name misused on television, by other children and sometimes by adults with whom they come into contact. Planning a worship time can help the children understand the meaning of reverence.

PLAN A WORSHIP TIME

In large group, discuss the first four commandments and what they should mean to us as we worship.

1. Thou shalt have no other gods before me. (God should come first in our lives. Ask how they can be sure this is true in their lives.)
2. Thou shalt not make unto thee any graven image. (Idol worship is not widespread in our country, so you may need to explain that some people do worship idols. Pictures are often provided in missionary newsletters.)
3. Thou shalt not take the name of the Lord thy God in vain. (Remind the children to always speak God's name with love.)
4. Remember the sabbath day, to keep it holy. (The main business of Sunday, the Christian's day of worship, is to worship God.)

If you teach with one or more teachers, divide the children into small groups and assign each group part of the service: music, prayers, Bible reading, etc. Encourage the children to stress reverence for God in their service. Psalm 8, Psalm 19 and Psalm 47 are Scriptures which can be read as well as the first four commandments. The children might like to draw or paint pictures or a mural to illustrate reverence for God.

You may want to invite some adults or another class to participate in your worship service. Remind the children that they are not performing, but leading in worship.

Shining Star Publications, Copyright © 1988, A division of Good Apple, Inc.

SS847

BUTTONS, BANNERS AND BALLOONS

List the last six commandments on the chalk board. Ask the children to write them as slogans for buttons, banners or balloons. Make construction paper or poster board buttons and banners. Do the same with paper shaped balloons. Spend time discussing the meaning of any of the commandments the children do not understand.

5. Honour thy father and thy mother.
6. Thou shalt not kill.
7. Thou shalt not commit adultery. (Do not skip over this commandment. Children need to be taught early that God expects married people to be faithful to each other.)
8. Thou shalt not steal.
9. Thou shalt not bear false witness against thy neighbour.
10. Thou shalt not covet.

THE TEN COMMANDMENTS SAID .... JESUS SAID .... OUR LAWS TODAY

The activity sheet, on page 22, can be done as a group, but older or more advanced students can do it as an individual project. For very young students, the teacher can do the reading while the children decide if Jesus was saying the same thing as the commandment. In the section about today's laws, simply ask the children if they know a law that corresponds with a commandment. To get started, give several examples.

Shining Star Publications, Copyright © 1988, A division of Good Apple, Inc. SS847

THE TEN COMMANDMENTS SAID .... JESUS SAID .... OUR LAWS TODAY

The Ten Commandments in Exodus 20 read:	Jesus said:	Today's laws say:
1. Thou shalt have no other gods before me.	Mark 12:30	
2. Thou shalt not make unto thee any graven image.	Matthew 6:33; John 4:24	
3. Thou shalt not take the name of the Lord thy God in vain.	Matthew 5:34,35	
4. Remember the sabbath day, to keep it holy.	Matthew 12:8; Mark 2:27, 28; 3:4	
5. Honour thy father and thy mother.	Matthew 15:4-9	
6. Thou shalt not kill.	Matthew 5:21,22	
7. Thou shalt not commit adultery.	Matthew 5:28,29	
8. Thou shalt not steal.	Matthew 19:18	
9. Thou shalt not bear false witness against thy neighbour.	Matthew 19:18	
10. Thou shalt not covet.	Luke 12:13-15	

Are there laws today about this?

THE TEN COMMANDMENTS

PLAQUES

To create a beautiful plaque you will need copies of the Ten Commandments and a piece of wood slightly larger. Duplicate the Ten Commandments in calligraphy, found below, on brown paper for each student.

Tearing the paper along the edge will give the plaque a nice look. Let the children sand their piece of wood and attach the paper with glue or paste. To preserve the plaque, a plastic fixative should be added later.

WALL HANGINGS

Help your students make this memory aid to celebrate the Ten Commandments. Collect plastic snap-on lids so each child has ten matching ones. Have children type or print each commandment on a circle of construction paper, cut to fit inside the plastic lids. Children are to glue a circle inside each lid. Then glue the lids in order, to a wide piece of ribbon. A "D" ring or a bow attached to the top will give the project a finished look.

...THE TEN COMMANDMENTS...

1. Thou shalt have no other gods before me.
2. Thou shalt not make unto thee any graven image.
3. Thou shalt not take the name of the Lord thy God in vain.
4. Remember the sabbath day, to keep it holy.
5. Honor thy father and thy mother.
6. Thou shalt not kill.
7. Thou shalt not commit adultery.
8. Thou shalt not steal.
9. Thou shalt not bear false witness against thy neighbor.
10. Thou shalt not covet.

WHAT ABOUT MOSES?

STAGES OF MOSES' LIFE

Encourage the children to do some simple research into the life of Moses. Divide the class into three groups, each studying a different stage of his life, or study each stage all together.

Group I—The first 40 years
1. Where was Moses born? Exodus 1—2:2
2. What important thing happened to him while he was a baby? Exodus 2:2-9
3. Why did Moses leave Egypt? Exodus 2:11-15

Group II—The second 40 years
1. After Moses left Egypt where did he go? Exodus 2:15
2. Who did Moses marry? Exodus 2:21
3. Who was his father-in-law? Exodus 3:1
4. What was his job? Exodus 3:1
5. How did God change his life? Exodus 3:2-10
6. Who did God give Moses as a helper? Exodus 3:14
7. Did Pharoah let God's people leave Egypt?

Group III—The third 40 years
1. What was given by God to Moses on Mount Sinai? Exodus 20
2. Did the Israelites always please God? Exodus 32:1-14
3. How old was Moses when he died? Deuteronomy 34:7

THE LIFE OF MOSES

Have several of the children dress up as Moses, Aaron, Miriam, Moses' mother and/or father, Jethro, Zipporah, the pharaoh, some of the Israelites, etc.

Let the other children plan, in order, introductions for each of these. This group should choose one of their members to be the master of ceremonies. Encourage "Moses" to talk to the various characters as they appear.

CHARACTER DOLLS

In a variation of the above, borrow "fashion" dolls and let the children dress them as Moses and the characters in his life. Beards can be temporarily fixed to the men's faces with Plasti-Tac. Much of the clothing can be made by simply cutting and belting.

A display could be made by standing the dolls in clay and printing information about each person on an index card to be placed in front of each doll.

Shining Star Publications, Copyright © 1988, A division of Good Apple, Inc. SS847

TEN COMMANDMENTS
Music by Helen Friesen

God told His peo-ple, "I'm the Lord your God, I brought you out of E-gypt. You shall have no oth-er gods. Make no grav-en im-age, nor bow down to it, for I am a jeal-ous God, lov-ing those who wor-ship me. You shall not mis-use my name. Keep the Sab-bath ho- - ly, for six days you may la-bor and do all your work. Hon-or your fa-ther, and hon-or your moth-er too. You shall not mur-der, nor com-mit a-dul-ter-y. You shall not steal or lie a-bout your neigh-bor; nor shall you cov-et his house, nor an-y-thing that is his. Keep my com-mand-ments, for then my love will flow un-to your chil-dren's chil - - - dren, just as I have prom-ised you.

THE TEN COMMANDMENTS AND DAILY LIVING

ROLE-PLAY

Ask for volunteers to act out the following situations. Remind them to use what they have learned about the Ten Commandments in responding to the problems. After the role-play, ask the group what commandment was involved in each situation.

1. Two boys, Bob and Sam, are standing in a toy store looking at a small car. Bob says he would like to have it. Sam suggests Bob slip it under his jacket while he distracts the sales clerk.
2. Mother tells Mary to set the table for supper. Mary is playing with her dolls and thinks if she pretends not to hear, Mother will do the job for her.
3. Tommy and Jim are fighting. Dad tells them to go to their rooms to calm down. Tommy becomes angry and starts to tell his dad, "No."
4. Beth does not like her next door neighbor, Mrs. Simmons, because she always complains to Beth's mother about the noise all the children make. Another neighbor, Mrs. Little, is angry because someone picked flowers from her garden. Beth thinks she could get even with Mrs. Simmons if she told Mrs. Little she had seen Mrs. Simmons pick the flowers. Beth really had not seen Mrs. Simmons pick the flowers.

VISITOR

Ask a policeman, security officer, lawyer or judge to speak to the children about how much easier (or unnecessary) their jobs would be if everyone followed the teachings in the Ten Commandments. (Be sure the person you invite knows the age and attention span of your group.)

THANK YOU

Explain to the children that honoring their parents means more than just obeying them. Ask them to suggest positive ways they can show honor to their parents. Provide paper and pencils and ask them to write thank-you notes to their parents. (If your class has younger children you may need to let them dictate their notes to you.)

FIELD TRIPS

MEETING MOSES AT THE MALL

Do not fill your children in on your planned activities for this field trip. Let them guess from the title. If the mall or shopping center is crowded, you will probably have more success walking around in small groups led by well-informed adults.

As soon as you arrive, ask the children to look for things in the mall which would not be necessary if people followed the Ten Commandments all the time. (Locks, security guards, detection devices, etc.)

If possible, arrange beforehand for a store manager or security person to talk to the children about all the trouble and expense caused by shoplifting (stealing). He might show them some of the ways they try to stop it. If there is a security office at the mall, check to see if the children can see it.

A movie theater might have posters which show people breaking some of the commandments. Some of your children may notice this and want to discuss it. Be prepared!

Have someone dressed as Moses meet the group for refreshments at the end of their mall walk. (Check this out with management before you arrive. If that cannot be worked out, Moses could meet them in the parking lot or back at the school or church building.) Let him ask the children to share what they have learned.

VISIT A COURTROOM

Visiting an actual trial probably would be hard to arrange and many trials would be upsetting to the children. However, the atmosphere of most courtrooms is impressive, so a visit to the courthouse might prove valuable. Call the courthouse and ask, explaining the age and size of your group as well as your purpose.

Explain to the children that many things happening in a courtroom are not pleasant, but most could be avoided if people followed the Ten Commandments.

LOCAL TREASURES

Most of us cannot travel hundreds of miles for a field trip. There may be something special in your own backyard.

For example, near Murphy, North Carolina, at Fields of the Woods (704-494-7855) there is a display of the largest Ten Commandments in the world. The individual letters are five feet high and four feet wide. It is an impractical trip for most children's groups, but a wonderful one for those who live nearby.

Check museums, churches, seminaries, etc. for displays that might add to your group's understanding of what they have studied.

PERMISSION SLIP

My child _____

has permission to participate in a field trip

to _____

with _____.

Phone number where parent can be reached

_____

Alternate number _____

Signed _____

Date _____

- -

Time leaving _____ Returning _____

Contact person: _____

Shining Star Publications, Copyright © 1988, A division of Good Apple, Inc. SS847

THE BIBLE TEACHES US ABOUT KINGS

Familiarize your children with three biblical kings, Saul, David and Solomon. Lead them to understand the unique qualities each man demonstrated as he ruled his kingdom, with the activities in this chapter.

Bulletin Board Idea

KING OF KINGS

PURPOSE: To remind boys and girls that even though royalty, fame and riches may seem glamorous, knowing Jesus is the greatest treasure of all.

PROCEDURE:
1. Cover the board with the richest purple material you can obtain. Purple velvet would be ideal.
2. Use an overhead projector to enlarge the treasure chest on brown paper. Using a black marker, draw lines on treasure chest to resemble wood grain, hinges and lock.
3. Reproduce the coin pattern on page 30 for each child. Follow directions on same page to make coins.

Shining Star Publications, Copyright © 1988, A division of Good Apple, Inc.   SS847

KING OF KINGS COIN

JESUS IS KING OF KINGS

BACK SIDE OF COIN

1. Cut out coin and mount on light cardboard.
2. Put a line of white glue along each letter on coin and attach pieces of string to each letter. (This procedure will make raised letters.)
3. Put aside until completely dry.
4. Cover coin with a piece of gold or aluminum foil, and fold neatly in the back. Glue edges of foil to the back of the coin.
5. Press the foil around the lettering to accent the words, before the glue on back side of coin dries.
6. Coins can be rubbed with black shoe polish to accent the raised letters.
7. Attach coins to the bulletin board.

FINGERPLAYS AND A SONG OF KINGS

KING SAUL

"Give us a king," the people cried,
(Hold up five fingers left hand.)

So God sent to them King Saul.
(One finger right hand.)

"You and your king must obey my law,"
(Move both hands slightly.)

God warned, "Or you will fall."
(Put all fingers down.)

THREE KINGS

Tell the children that each time you point to them they should say, "Saul, David, Solomon."

There were three kings in Israel land.
Refrain: "Saul, David, Solomon"

God chose them all to fulfill His plan.
Refrain:

When they ruled well, life was good.
Refrain:

But they forgot God's teachings, as He knew they would.
Refrain:

Forgetting brought unhappiness, obeying brought them joy.
Refrain:

Obeying is always better for a king or girl or boy.
Refrain:

YOUTHFUL DAVID
Words and Music by Helen Friesen

[Musical notation with lyrics:]
1. David, the son of Jesse, lived in his home near Bethlehem. Samuel looked at those seven sons, but God said it was none of them. "Have you no other sons but these?" "Yes," answered Jesse, "there is one, He tends the flocks of sheep I own." "Send for him now, I must see that son."

VERSE 2
David was called a handsome lad; God told the prophet, "He's the one."
Samuel anointed God's choice for a king; then he went home, for the deed was done.
"David," said Jesse, "take this food. Go find your brothers with King Saul."
When David reached the army camp, he saw a man nearly ten feet tall.

VERSE 3
King Saul was troubled, plain to see. "Who will do battle with this man?"
"If he succeeds, I'll reward him well." David stepped forth, "I will fight this man."
Picking his way to the stream below, he found five stones that pleased him well.
Armed with his slingshot David went; my, how the mighty giant fell.

SOMETHING TO SING ABOUT

"... the glorious majesty of his kingdom." Psalms 145:12

COMPOSING

Let the children try their hands at putting verses from one of David's psalms to music. If you have access to a piano or small keyboard, learn the tunes to some familiar songs: "Row, Row, Row, Your Boat", "Mary Had a Little Lamb", etc. For example, the first two verses of Psalm 29 fit well to the tune of "Mary Had a Little Lamb."

> Give unto the Lo-r-d,
> O-O-O, ye mighty,
> Give unto the Lo-r-d,
> glory and strength.
> Give unto the Lo-r-d
> the glory due unto His name;
> W-o-rship the Lo-r-d,
> in the beauty of holiness.

Remind the children that David first served Saul as a musician to quiet his troubled spirit. Play different types of music (on an instrument or play a tape) for the children and let them decide which is most comforting.

If there is a piano, small keyboard and/or melody bells available to your children, let them make up simple songs. You may be surprised at how well they do. Perhaps you can tape some of their compositions.

RHYTHM INSTRUMENTS

If possible, provide rhythm instruments for the children to use in experiencing rhythm in music. These can be used as they listen to recordings.

MUSICAL

If you or one of your co-teachers is especially musical, perhaps you would like to help your class put together a musical about the first three kings of Israel.

Use songbooks designed for young children to find songs about the kings. These could be alternated with some of the fingerplays and song found on page 31, facts about the kings and dialogue. The children can work on staging and, perhaps, costuming.

Share the musical with other classes or parents.

KINGS CHART

"The Lord reigneth...." Psalms 99:1

Cover a piece of heavy cardboard with a flannel-type material, in a light color. Using the chart shown below, print the numbers of the first three kings in black; print the numbers of the kings of Judah in red; and print the numbers of the kings of Israel, after the division, in purple. Draw a rough outline of the kingdoms of Judah and Israel between the lines showing the division. Cut rectangles from flannel for each of the kings. Print the names of the first three in black and number them. Print the names of the kings of Judah in red; and print the names of the kings of Israel, after the division, in purple. If the children you are working with are old enough, let them help make the chart. If not, let them assemble it using the color and number codes. (This is a learning activity you may want to make available to other classes.)

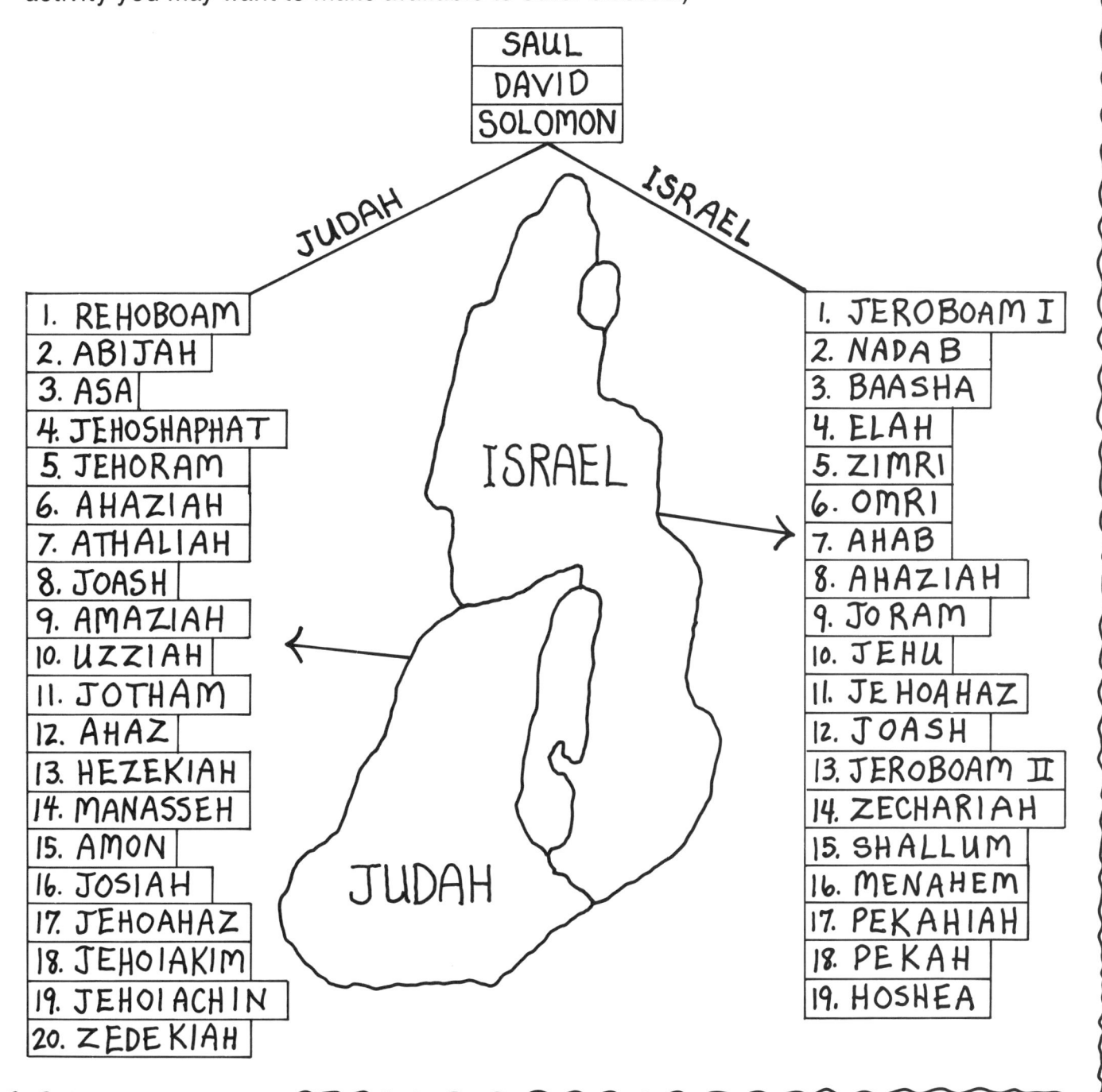

SAUL
DAVID
SOLOMON

JUDAH / ISRAEL

Judah:
1. REHOBOAM
2. ABIJAH
3. ASA
4. JEHOSHAPHAT
5. JEHORAM
6. AHAZIAH
7. ATHALIAH
8. JOASH
9. AMAZIAH
10. UZZIAH
11. JOTHAM
12. AHAZ
13. HEZEKIAH
14. MANASSEH
15. AMON
16. JOSIAH
17. JEHOAHAZ
18. JEHOIAKIM
19. JEHOIACHIN
20. ZEDEKIAH

Israel:
1. JEROBOAM I
2. NADAB
3. BAASHA
4. ELAH
5. ZIMRI
6. OMRI
7. AHAB
8. AHAZIAH
9. JORAM
10. JEHU
11. JEHOAHAZ
12. JOASH
13. JEROBOAM II
14. ZECHARIAH
15. SHALLUM
16. MENAHEM
17. PEKAHIAH
18. PEKAH
19. HOSHEA

PICTURE SEQUENCING

Read each Scripture verse and put the pictures in order by placing the appropriate number in each box.

Saul offering the burnt offering.
I Samuel 13:8-14

Samuel anoints Saul king.
I Samuel 10:1

Saul sent out by his father to look for the lost donkeys. I Samuel 9:3

David offers to fight Goliath.
I Samuel 17:32-51

Saul dies.
I Samuel 31:1-6

Saul being made king at Gilgal.
I Samuel 11:15

CREATIVE WRITING

Purchase primary manuscript paper. At the top of each sheet, print one of the following open-ended sentences:

A good king should be . . . .
A good king always . . . .
One law a good king should make is . . . .
People should be able to see their king . . . .
People should be able to talk to their king . . . .
A king should be given . . . .
People need a king because . . . .

Ask children to complete their sentences. You may need to serve as secretary for the younger children. Read (with the children's permission) each finished thought.

POETRY

Write the words "A king should be" on the chalkboard. List things the children name underneath.

A king should be_____

_____

_____

Let the children name words that rhyme with king. Working a line at a time, help the class create a poem.

GROUP STORY

Have the group write a story about a king who believed in God and wanted his people to obey God. Let each child contribute a line to the story. Have a co-teacher quickly write down the story or use a tape recorder.

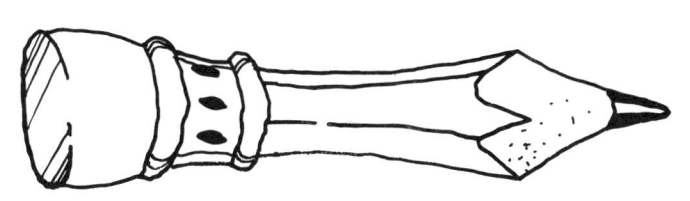

DESCRIPTIVE WORDS

Write the names of Saul, David and Solomon in the middle of large pieces of construction paper. Divide the children into three groups.

Ask each group to think of as many words as they can to describe the king named on their sheet of paper.

SHARING

You will want to keep a copy of poems and stories your children create on various topics. Once or twice a year print them in a newsletter or small booklet so they can be shared with parents.

PROJECT PAGE

"When the righteous are in authority, the people rejoice...."   Proverbs 29:2

King Solomon was a builder. His two chief buildings were the temple which took seven years to build and his own palace which took thirteen years to complete. Many elaborate reconstructions of the temple have been done. Using the simple outline given, your class can do its own reconstruction.

Before building, explain to the children:
1. God would not allow David to build the temple because he was a man of war.
2. The temple was based on the same pattern as the tabernacle built soon after the Ten Commandments were given.
3. The temple was twice as big as the tabernacle and three times as tall.

Read I Kings 6 to the children. Ask them to listen for the types of materials used and the things that were to be placed in the temple.

Find pictures of reconstructions of the temple (Bible dictionaries or encyclopedias) to show the children, but tell them you do not expect their model to be as detailed.

Sugar cubes and glue, craft sticks with glue and tape (takes paint well, but might give impression of a wild west fort), or clay can be used in the construction.

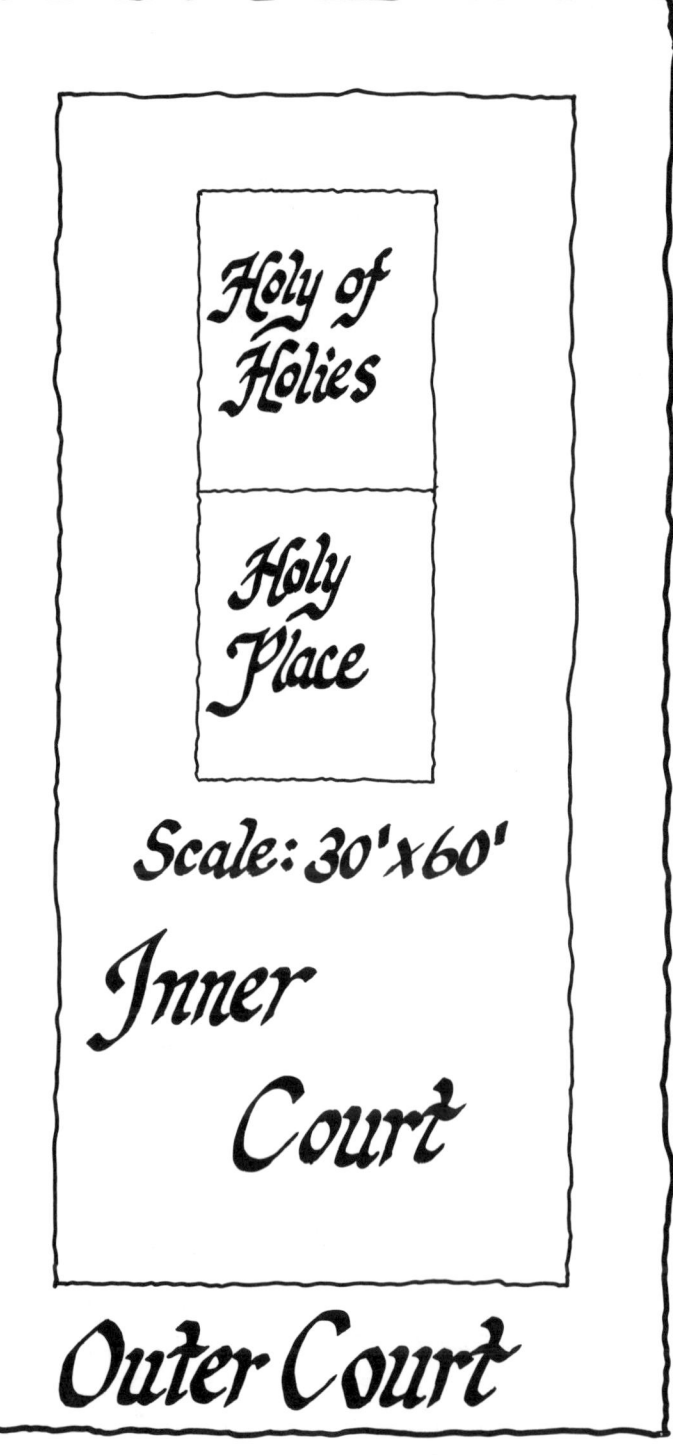

Holy of Holies

Holy Place

Scale: 30' x 60'

Inner Court

Outer Court

Shining Star Publications, Copyright © 1988, A division of Good Apple, Inc.   SS847

HOW MANY?

Solomon had a large household. Trace the patterns below, cut out and print the Scripture references on each. Give each child a pattern (you may need to duplicate) and let them look up the amount of food it took to feed Solomon's household for the day. Ask the children to share their findings and then glue their outlines on a poster board labeled, "COME TO DINNER." You may need to help locate Scriptures and translate measurements (example: threescore = 60).

I Kings 4:22
Flour

I Kings 4:23
Fat oxen

I Kings 4:22
Meal

I Kings 4:23
Fowl

I Kings 4:23
Sheep

I Kings 4:23
Oxen out of pasture

I Kings 4:23
Fallowdeer

I Kings 4:23
Harts

I Kings 4:23
Roebucks

WANTED

Lead the children to understand that God carefully selected the men He chose to be king over his people. But these men were not always faithful to God after becoming king.

WANT ADS

Print the following job description on the board and help the children fill in the blanks.

A man who _____.

(I Samuel 8:3,5) A_____

_____. (I Samuel 13:14)

Salary: _____

(I Samuel 8:11-17)

BRAINSTORMING

Our children are more likely to be familiar with presidents than with kings. Let them brainstorm things they think make a good president.

INTERVIEWS

In three small groups (or together as a large group) study the qualifications of Saul, David and Solomon.

Saul: I Samuel 9:1,2,15,16; 10:17-24; 11
David: I Samuel 16:1-13; 17:40-51;
II Samuel 2:1-4
Solomon: I Kings 1:30-40; 2:1-4

Let the children choose one of their group to play a job interviewer and one to play the king whose qualifications they studied. Set the stage as Saul, David and Solomon apply for the job as king.

After all three role-plays, let the children decide which of the three they think was most qualified and which was the best king.

SAUL

DAVID

SOLOMON

THE TOOLS OF DAVID

Find and circle the hidden objects David may have used during his life.

ROYAL PARTY

Plan a party with the decorations, games, foods and devotional ideas that follow to reinforce what the children have learned about the three kings.

DECORATIONS

If possible, let the children make some of the decorations for the party.

THESE MAY INCLUDE:
SILVER TRAYS: trays or cardboard covered with foil
Silver bowls: plastic bowls covered in the same way.
ROYAL CRESTS: Ask the children to glue cording onto large pieces of cardboard, cover loosely with foil and gently press around design.

Other decorations can be made using deep purple crepe paper. Large sheets make wonderful table coverings. If your tables can be lowered, do so and let the children recline on borrowed throw pillows.

INVITATIONS

Each child should be given an invitation.
Example:

Hear ye, Hear ye:

_____(name of child)_____

is invited to a royal banquet on

_____(date)_____

from ____(time)____ until ____(time)____.

at _____(place)_____

All guests are invited to come dressed as a member of royalty from any time period.

PRESENTATIONS

Have an adult in appropriate costume stationed at the door to announce each royal guest to the crowd. (Of course, the royal guest will have to tell the adult who he or she is representing.)

ROYAL RINGTOSS

Foil-covered rings can be used for the traditional ringtoss game.

PIN THE JEWELS ON THE CROWN

Use gold stickers or stars on a silver crown. You should use a velvet blindfold.

ROYAL TREASURE HUNT

Estimate the number of guests beforehand. Divide into teams of three or four. Write clues for each team, leading to the hidden treasure (a decorated box of gold foil-covered candy). Encourage the winners to be generous royalty and share.

ROYAL BANQUET

Ask the announcer to invite guests to be seated at the banquet table. Servants are to be dressed in costumes. Announce each course and serve.

Menu might include:
Royal Fruit Delight (fruit cocktail cup)

Coronation Broth (tomato soup)

Covered Roasted Fowl (turkey frank in bun)

Majestic Frozen Confection
(scoop of ice cream sprinkled with colored sugar)

DEVOTIONAL

You may want to end the royal party something like this:

"I am sure it has been fun for you to pretend to be royalty today."

"Though none of us are kings or queens, we are pretty special because we do know a king. Can you tell me who that king is? (Let the children answer.) That's right, Jesus is our King of kings." Rev. 17:14

"Even though it may feel pretty special to be treated like royalty, I would rather be a servant of the King of kings, than be an earthly king myself. How about you?"

THE BIBLE TEACHES US HOW TO PRAISE GOD

Bulletin Board Idea

GARDEN OF PRAISES

PURPOSE: To encourage children to research the Bible for verses of praise.

PROCEDURE:
1. Cover top half of bulletin board with sky-blue paper and bottom half with white paper. Using a sponge and green paint, dab the paint-soaked sponge on the bottom half of the board to make "grass."
2. Reproduce the flower blooms, found on page 42, for each child on different colors of construction paper.
3. Children are to use their Bibles to find verses about praise. Depending on the age of your students, you may want to give some Scripture references on the chalkboard. After children locate Bible verses on praise, they are to print the verses in the center of blossoms. Then color or paint the flowers and "plant" in the Praise Garden by attaching it to the bulletin board. Use wide-tip markers to add stems and leaves to the blossoms.

ADDITIONAL ACTIVITY: After bulletin board is covered with praise flowers, let the children use fine-tip black markers to add spiders, ants, butterflies, etc. to the garden.

BIBLICAL REFERENCES FOR PRAISE

Revelation 7:12, 4:11, 1:5,6, 19:1-6
Psalms 68:35, 148:1, 52:9, 148:2, 66:2, 34:1, 63:4, 100:4, 145:21, 72:19, 149:1, 9:1, 34:1, 150:6, 67:3, 9:2, 145:1, 106:48, 68:32, 66:20, 145:2, 113:2, 103:1, 146:2, 113:3, 107:8, 111:1, 68:19, 86:12

Judges 5:3
Nehemiah 9:5
I Timothy 1:17, 6:15,16
Luke 24:53

GARDEN OF PRAISES PATTERNS

USING OUR MOUTH FOR LEARNING

MOTHER, MAY I?

Teacher gives directions to individual pupils. Example: Take two giant steps. Pupil must ask, "Mother, (or Teacher) may I?" before attempting the task.

TELEPHONE

Group sits in a circle. The teacher whispers a biblical phrase to the child sitting beside him. That pupil repeats what he thinks he heard to the next pupil, and so on. The last pupil must say what he thinks he heard to the teacher.

OBJECT LESSON

Take a handful of feathers or shredded (biodegradable, please) tissue. Go to the window (this works better on a windy day) and toss them outside. As your students stare in horror, tell them you want them to go outside and gather all the feathers or pieces of tissue. When they have been unsuccessful in doing this, remind them that careless words are even harder to retrieve.

DISCUSSION STARTERS

1. I am most likely to say something I should not when . . . .
2. I do not like for people to talk about . . . .
3. When I feel unhappy the person I most like to talk to is . . . .
4. I find it hard to talk about . . . .
5. I find it easy to talk about . . . .
6. When someone I love is feeling sad I usually . . . .

BRAINSTORMING

Give each child a sheet of paper with the word "MOUTH" written in the middle. Ask the children to write every word that "MOUTH" makes them think of on the paper. If you have a young class, do this as a group activity.

MEMORIZATION

Print the following Scriptures on strips of paper. Duplicates are fine, just be sure to have at least as many strips as you have pupils. Let each pupil choose one. Tell them a memorized verse by the next class meeting will entitle them to a reward. For the sake of those who will lose their strips keep a list. Some suggested Scriptures are:

Psalm 19:14
Matthew 5:37
Psalm 31:1
Psalm 141:3
Proverbs 10:31
Proverbs 21:23

See page 41 for additional Scripture verses.

Prizes may include: wax lips, Chap Stick or sugarless gum.

CREATIVE WRITING

"The lip of truth shall be established for ever...."   Proverbs 12:19

Using the outline below, ask pupils to write two stories: one about a child who always tells the truth, the other about a child who lies.

Introduction
I. Problem arises
II. Way problem is dealt with
Conclusion

You be the scribe and take down the story or record it. If you have a co-teacher and a fairly large class, why not let one group write one story and another the other? Sharing them will be fun. As the children compose their stories, you may need to ask guiding questions. For example:
What might happen that would make someone your age feel like telling a lie?
Is it always easy to tell the truth?
Is it ever right to tell a lie?

POETRY

Challenge the children to fill in the blanks below to make the poem their own. You might like to copy it on a chalk board so several variations can be easily tried.

My mouth can be_____.

My mouth can be_____.

How I use it
can make others _____.

After experimenting with the poem above, encourage the children to try writing their own. Have a brainstorming session beforehand and list rhyming words and ideas about the use of the tongue and mouth. Older children may want to work alone on a poem while younger ones will probably prefer to work as a group.

JOURNALS

Help the children to make a little notebook by fastening notebook pages between two sheets of construction paper. Encourage them to keep a list, for a week, of the nice things people say to them, and the nice things they say to others.

Shining Star Publications, Copyright © 1988, A division of Good Apple, Inc.

SS847

CRAFTS

"Righteous lips are the delight of kings . . . ." Proverbs 16:13

POTATO HEADS

Using a potato, apple or orange as a base, let the children fashion faces with cloves, seeds or candies.

Discuss why some mouths always seem happy, while others always seem sad.

BIG MOUTH CADDY

Provide a one-gallon milk jug for each child. Before class, cut out large "mouths" as shown. From felt, cut "eyes" and "noses." Let the children glue these in place, cover the outside of lid with a strip of felt, and cut and glue a cap bill to the bottom of lid.

Tell the children that they should use their Big Mouth Caddy to hold things such as lunch money, pencils and other things they need to remember to take to school. A little organization sometimes helps to avoid angry words.

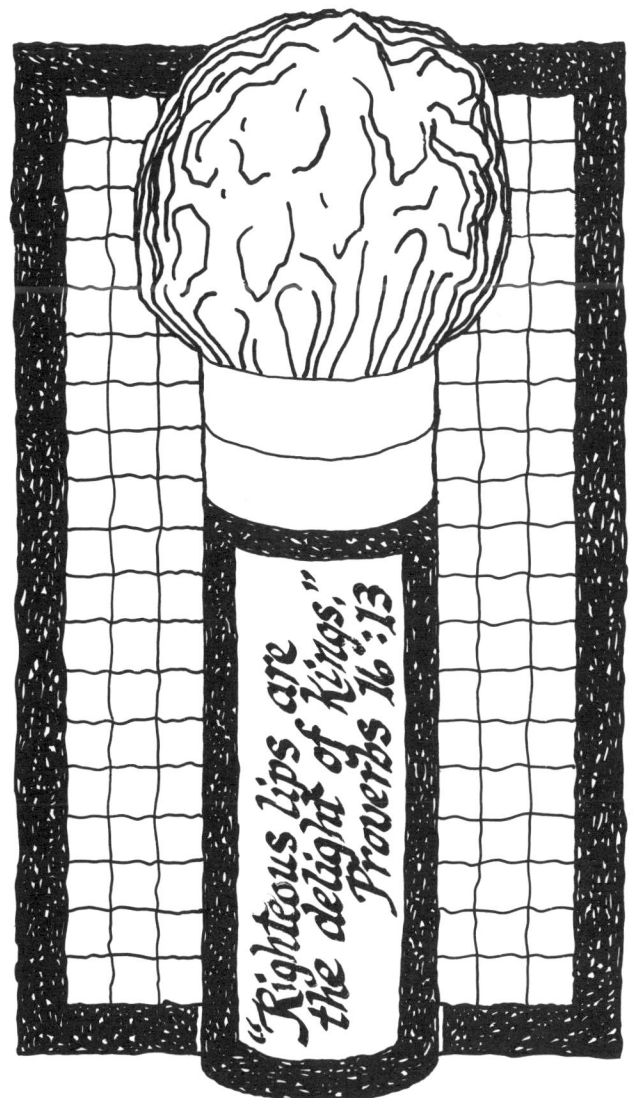

PRAISE MICROPHONES

Give each child a paper towel tube, a sheet of newspaper, a 4" x 4" piece of aluminum foil and tape. Demonstrate how a play microphone can be made by wadding the newspaper into a ball, covering the ball with aluminum foil, and taping it to the top of the paper towel tube. The tube can be painted black and an appropriate Bible verse taped on it.

Use the play microphones to read praise Scriptures. (See page 41 for Scriptures.)

Shining Star Publications, Copyright © 1988, A division of Good Apple, Inc.   SS847

LET'S COOK

"Whoso keepeth his mouth and his tongue keepeth his soul from troubles."
Proverbs 21:23

SCRIPTURE DROPS

Combine the suggested amounts of the ingredients found in the listed Bible verses, to make Scripture drops.

1 part I Samuel 14:25
3 parts Judges 5:25 (dried)
1 part I Samuel 30:12

Place in refrigerator or cool place for a few minutes.

EASY COOKING

Any of the following can be prepared in a classroom situation:
instant pudding—use a shaker jar or bowl and egg beater
refrigerator cookie, bread dough, small cake or bread mixes—use a toaster oven or church kitchen
instant rice—(be careful of hot water)

While the children are sampling their efforts, it is a wonderful time for teaching Bible truths.

TASTING PARTY

Choose at least five of the following to serve at your tasting party: nuts, raisins, carrot sticks, celery sticks, marshmallows, dry cereal, apple slices, orange sections, warm lemon slices.

Discuss texture, sweetness, sourness, etc.

CONVERSATION STARTERS

"The Bible tells us what comes out of our mouths can do us more harm than putting the wrong things in our mouths. Still we should be careful to care for our bodies by putting only clean, wholesome food in them."

"Can you tell me one thing you should always do before cooking?"

"There are many different foods in the world. What are your favorites?"

"If you could have only one food for an entire month, what would it be?"

Shining Star Publications, Copyright © 1988, A division of Good Apple, Inc.

SS847

CLAP AND PRAISE
AN EXERCISE SONG
Words by Helen Kitchell Evans
Music by Frances Mann Benson

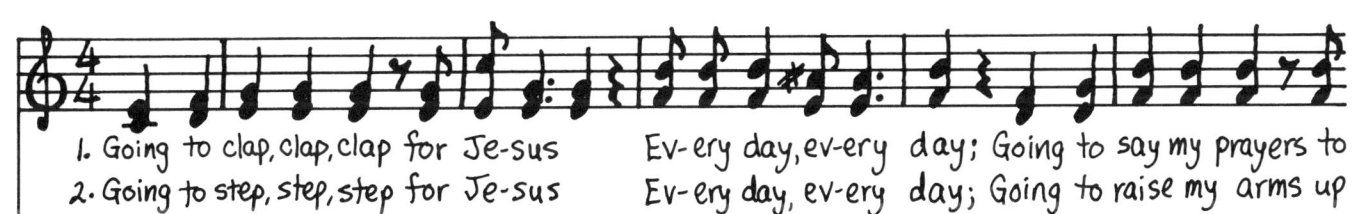

1. Going to clap, clap, clap for Jesus Ev-ery day, ev-ery day; Going to say my prayers to Je-sus Ev-ery day, Ev-ery day. Going to swing my arms wide o-pen And hug dear Jesus ver-y tight For He's my bless-ed Sav-ior who helps me day and night.

2. Going to step, step, step for Jesus Ev-ery day, ev-ery day; Going to raise my arms up high And pray, pray, pray Ev-ery day. Going to praise my lov-ing sav-ior, The One who cares so much for me For Je-sus makes me hap-py, as hap-py as can be.

Going to *clap, clap, clap* for Jesus (Clap hands three times.)
Every *day, every day;* (Clap hands on *day*.)
Going to say my prayers to Jesus (Swings arms over head.)
Every day, every day. (Hold hands in prayerful position.)
Going to swing my arms wide open (Open arms wide with shoulders back.)
And hug dear Jesus very tight (Bring arms over chest in a hugging position.)
For He's my blessed Savior (Hold above position.)
Who helps me day and night.

Going to *step, step, step* for Jesus (Step on left foot, then right, then left.)
Every *day, every day;* (Step right on *day*, left on second *day*.)
Going to raise my arms up high (Put arms up and reach for the sky.)
And *pray, pray, pray*—every *day*.
(Bend elbows slightly and raise hands three times on *pray, pray, pray*.
Hold at waist on *every day*.)
Going to praise my loving Savior, (Touch head on *going*.)
The One who cares for *me* (Touch chest *on me*.)
For Jesus makes me happy, (Move arms up and down, just as fast as possible, not in rhythm.)
As happy as can be.)

Shining Star Publications, Copyright © 1988, A division of Good Apple, Inc.

FIELD TRIP

"The mouth of the just bringeth forth wisdom . . . ."   Proverbs 10:31

Do you have a Christian radio or television station in your area? If so, why not plan a visit? Write a letter to the station manager asking if such a visit is possible. Do this well ahead of the time you plan to visit, giving at least two possible dates and expressing as much flexibility as possible. Explain the nature of your group, including the number of children and adults who will accompany them. State that you will call the station on a certain date for a response and to finalize arrangements if that response is positive.

At least a week before the trip, send home an information sheet and permission slip with each child. Arrange for transportation and adult helpers. The day before the field trip, telephone to remind parents of departure time and to bring permission slips.

Be sure to leave on time. Arriving at the station promptly will eliminate any schedule interruptions. Remind the children of the type of behavior you expect of them and tell them things to look for. The station personnel will be doing this as a favor, so remember to express gratitude. Taking a plate of cookies for the staff would be one way to say "Thanks."

After the field trip, have your class send a thank-you note or card.

Things to look for on field trip:
1. Before going, check programming and tell the children about programs they might be interested in. If you can do this a week or more ahead, the children will be able to view some of the programs.
2. Ask how many people watch or listen to this station or how far the station reaches.
3. Ask about programs which teach God's Word.
4. Ask about equipment which allows someone to teach thousands about Jesus at one time.
5. Ask about the cost of one program.

FOLLOW-UP

Have the children plan and "produce" a Christian television or radio program. This might be presented to a live audience or taped. Many people have video recorders, so a parent might be willing to tape a "television" program for the group.

ANOTHER FIELD TRIP

Visit a nursing home or individual shut-ins. Let the children use their mouths to bless these people with quiet conversation and singing.

Shining Star Publications, Copyright © 1988, A division of Good Apple, Inc.   SS847

MOUTH OF EXCELLENCE

"... his praise shall continually be in my mouth." Psalm 34:1

Do you have a dentist friend whom you could ask to talk to your class about the proper care of the mouth? If this is not possible, ask your dentist or check the library for booklets on dental hygiene.

A MODEL MOUTH

Draw a model like the one below on poster board or a chalkboard and have the children label the parts of the mouth: lips, teeth, tongue. Emphasize that God wants us to care for our physical mouth, but being careful about our "spiritual" mouth is important, too.

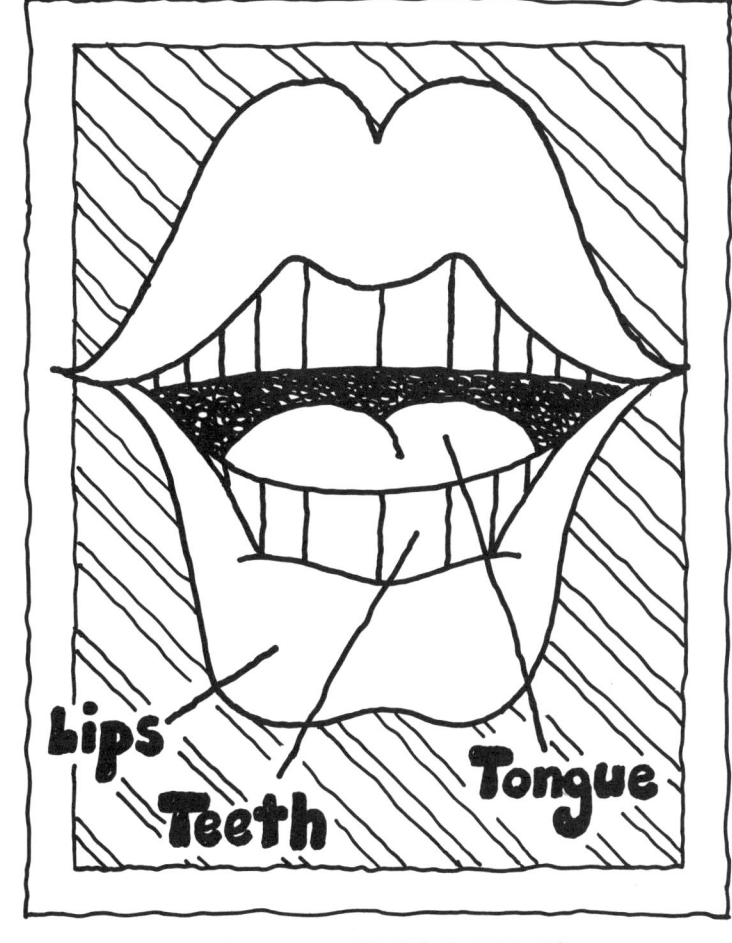

"... keep the door of my lips." Psalm 141:3

BATHROOM REMINDER

Using the toothbrush pattern, make one per child out of poster board. Let the children copy the Scripture, color the handle and glue pieces of heavy thread on bristle area. Use these mind jogglers as memory verse aids.

FILMSTRIPS

Check your local library for a filmstrip about dental care.

Shining Star Publications, Copyright © 1988, a division of Good Apple, Inc. SS847

PLAN A PRAISE PARTY

Everyone enjoys sincere praise. Often by the time a person has become an adult either shyness about giving praise or skill at giving insincere praise has become a habit. Why not plan a praise party to help your pupils practice praise? Of course, the practice can easily lead to a devotional time for praising God.

THE GATES OF PRAISE

Decorate the entry of the room where the praise party will be held. (This can be your regular classroom, a room in your home, etc.) Station someone outside the door to explain to the children that once they go through the "gates of praise" they are only supposed to say nice, complimentary things to people.

PRAISE BADGE

Pin a large paper heart on each child and give them a strip of stars, hearts or other stickers. Instruct the group that any time one person is given praise they are to put a sticker on that person's badge. Encourage the children to look for things they can be honest in praising, but do not be judgmental about what is honest praise and what is not.

PRAISE ACTIVITIES

1. Draw a large face on a sheet of poster board, leaving off the mouth. Cut smiling mouths from construction paper. Blindfold the children and give each a turn placing their paper smile in position. Once they have positioned the mouth it can be taped into place.
2. Wrap small, break-resistant mirrors for all the children. Before you pass them out, tell the children that their gift will help them see one of God's special children.

PRAISE CAKE

Make a sheet cake (it does not have to look like it came from a bakery) and letter it to read, "We Think You Are Special." Before serving, explain to the children that their teachers think they are each special people. Be as elaborate with the table decorations as possible, because we do special things for "special" people. Serve milk or juice with cake.

PRAISE PARTY DEVOTIONS

Find pictures of attractive men, women and children. Ask the children what they might praise or compliment about these people.

Find another group of pictures showing people doing kind, helpful things. Again ask what these people might be praised for. Emphasize the fact that the people in the first group might also deserve praise for some of the same type of things being done by those in the second group.

Now ask the children to name some things God should be praised for. Remind them that, like themselves, God enjoys being praised.

Lead the children in a praise song (see page 47) and prayer of praise.

Shining Star Publications, Copyright © 1988, A division of Good Apple, Inc. SS847

PUPPETS

Read Matthew 21:28-32 to your class.
Discuss: 1. Which son used his mouth wisely?
2. Is it better to say the right thing, do the right thing, or both?
3. Is saying that you will do something and then not doing it the same as lying?

Let the children decide how many puppets would be needed to act out this parable, what type of puppets should be made, and what type of stage would be needed. Use one of the suggested puppets below to share this story with another class.

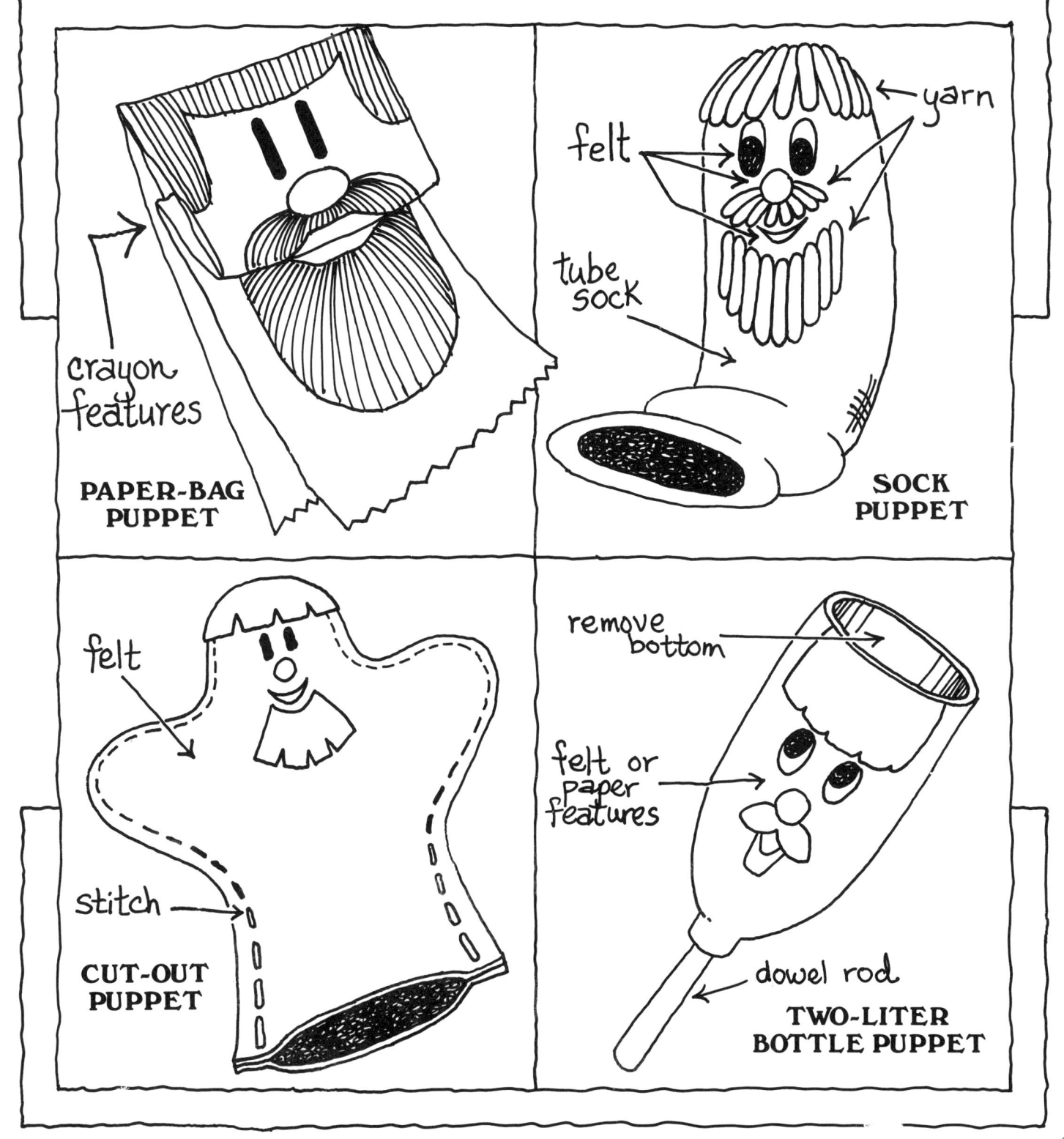

PAPER-BAG PUPPET — crayon features

SOCK PUPPET — yarn, felt, tube sock

CUT-OUT PUPPET — felt, stitch

TWO-LITER BOTTLE PUPPET — remove bottom, felt or paper features, dowel rod

WORKS OF ART

"Death and life are in the power of the tongue...." Proverbs 18:21

POSTER CONTEST

Suggest the children draw posters to explain a Scripture about praise. Give them several Scriptures to choose from. Give directions as to poster size and set a deadline. (This could be done within a class period with supplies being provided.) Recognition could be given for the poster which best illustrates the Scripture upon which it is based. (See praise Scripture references on page 41.)

The posters can be displayed in the church halls or at a special showing after youth meeting or church service some evening.

ART NIGHT

Write Proverbs 18:21, "Death and life are in the power of the tongue...," on your chalkboard. Ask the children to think about what it means. (If your class consists of mostly kindergarteners or first graders, you may want to choose a less powerful verse or have group discussion first.)

Set out several art mediums such as paint, colored chalk, paper, clay, chenille wires, crayons and fingerpaints. Let each of the children pick a medium with which to express their feelings.

GREETING CARDS

Remind the children that sometimes instead of saying things we must write them. Let them design greeting cards to cheer people. You may want to deliver these to a nursing home or to shut-ins.

Let the children suggest appropriate greetings, such as "Get Well Soon," "God Bless You," "Have a Happy Day." Write these on the chalkboard so they can be copied. Tell the children they are free to use their own greetings. Give them construction paper, glue, old greeting cards, crayons, markers and magazines to work with. Share the cards at the end of class and encourage the children to send their cards.

MURAL

Place a large strip of newsprint or wrapping paper along a wall. Let the children work with crayons or paints (be sure the wall won't be damaged) to create a mural about using the mouth in the way God would want them to. Discuss what the children feel should be included in the mural.

Shining Star Publications, Copyright © 1988, A division of Good Apple, Inc.   SS847

THE BIBLE TEACHES US HOW TO BE WISE

Helping children learn to use their Bibles to find answers to questions and solutions to problems is the greatest gift a teacher can give students. Lead your children on the path of truth with the games and activities that follow, all designed to make Bible learning fun.

Bulletin Board Idea

GOD IS LIGHT, IN HIM IS NO DARKNESS

PURPOSE: To demonstrate to youngsters that knowledge can "light" the world. Encourage cooperation and Scripture memory.

PROCEDURE:
1. Cover the bulletin board with black paper. Use an overhead projector to enlarge the planet earth, on blue paper. Cut out the letters from white paper and mount on bulletin board.
2. Reproduce enough copies of the stars, on page 54, so each child can have a dozen or more. Each time a Bible verse is memorized the child gets to write the verse on a star, sprinkle it lightly with glue and glitter and attach it to the bulletin board.
3. As the stars are attached to the board, the black background will disappear. How fast can your class "light" the world?

Shining Star Publications, Copyright © 1988, A division of Good Apple, Inc.   SS847

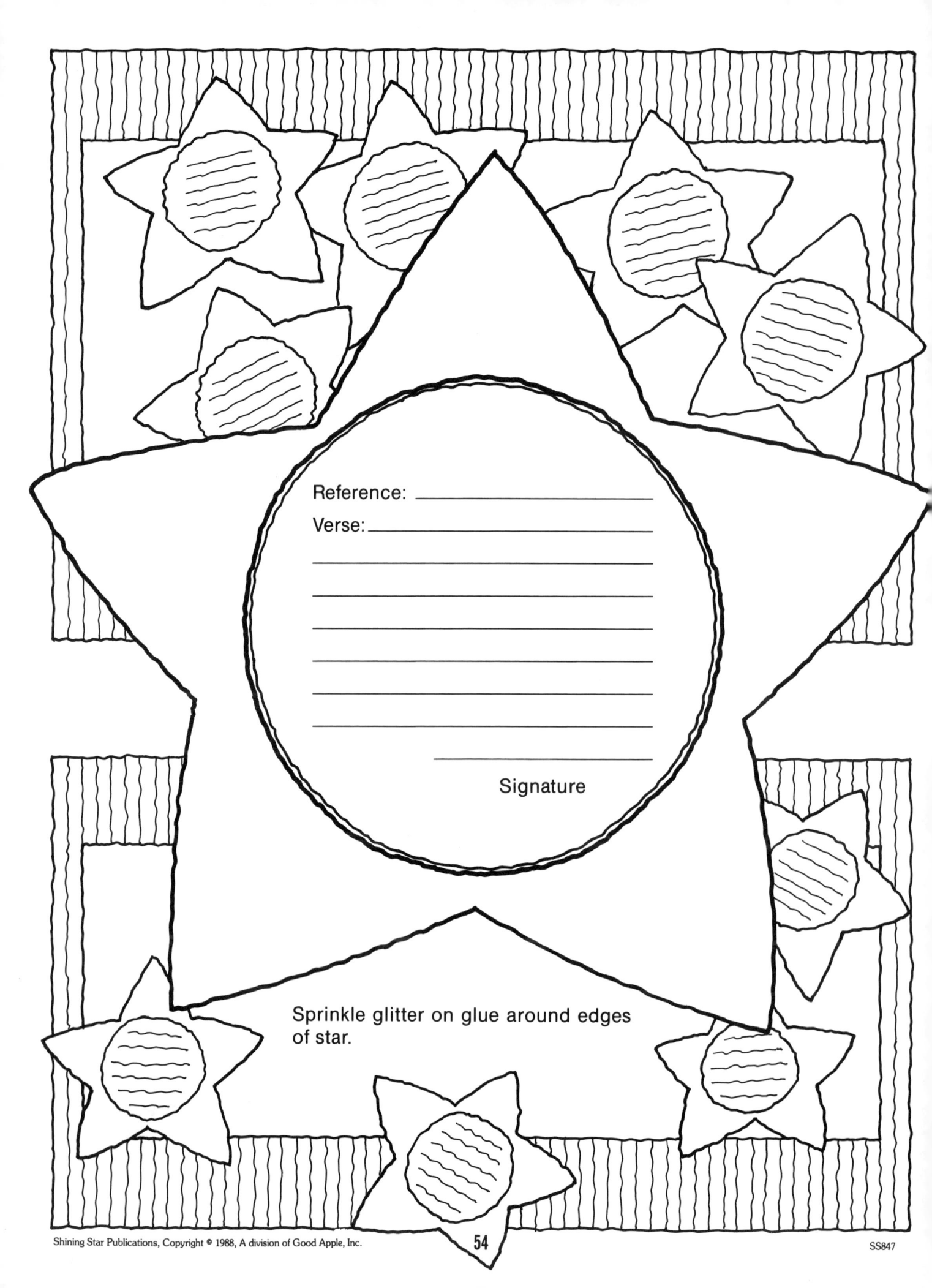

Reference: _____
Verse: _____
_____
_____
_____
_____
_____
_____
_____

Signature

Sprinkle glitter on glue around edges of star.

THE SOURCE OF WISDOM

FILL IN THE BLANKS

Write the following verses about wisdom on the chalkboard. Let the children find the references, either as small groups or as individuals, and fill in the blanks.

"A wise man will _____, and will increase _____; and a man of understanding shall attain unto wise counsels." Proverbs 1:5

"For the Lord _____ wisdom: out of his _____ cometh _____ and _____." Proverbs 2:6

"The wise shall _____ _____: but _____ shall be the promotion of fools." Proverbs 3:35

"For wisdom is better than _____; and all the things that may be desired are not to be compared to it." Proverbs 8:11

"The fear of the Lord is the _____ _____: and the knowledge of the _____ is understanding." Proverbs 9:10

MEMORY CONTRACTS

Prepare "Memory Contracts" for the children which read:
I, _____ promise to learn _____ by _____.
                          Signed _____

Let the children choose a verse from the list on the chalkboard. (If you have mostly older children, you may want to challenge them with longer passages, such as, Proverbs 2:1-6; Proverbs 7:2-4; or Proverbs 16:20-23.) When each child says the verse to you, mark their contract "fulfilled" and display it on poster board or bulletin board.

MEMORY DRILL

Print the words of each verse about wisdom you want the children to learn on 8" x 4" poster board cards. Divide the children into teams of two and let them work with each other learning one verse. As they begin to learn the verse, then their partner can wait for the next word before revealing the card. These cards can be used in the next two activities.

MEMORY SCRAMBLE

Using the memory drill cards described above, hand the words out and ask the children to arrange them in order. You may want to make sets of cards for each verse studied. As the group becomes more confident, they can work within a time limit.

These same cards can be used by individuals along the tray of the chalkboard, or on a table, to arrange the different verses in order. An egg timer can be used to challenge ability.

MEMORY PUZZLE

Print memory verses on cardboard or poster board. Cut around key words in an irregular manner. Ask the children to try to say the entire verse before putting the puzzle together.

MEMORY BEE

Divide the class into two teams. Alternating sides and members, let the children try to say the next word of a given verse. Do not use sitting down as punishment for missing a word, but give a point to the child's team for each correct word given.

Shining Star Publications, Copyright © 1988, A division of Good Apple, Inc.   SS847

DEMONSTRATING LOVE AT HOME

Let the children copy the following Scripture references on separate index cards. Encourage them to take the cards home to be read with their families.

Proverbs 3:1-10
Proverbs 4:1-4
Proverbs 6:20-23
Proverbs 22:6

You may want to send the following letter home as well.

Dear Parents,
We are learning about wisdom. As part of our study, we want to find out what the book of Proverbs has to say about families. The children are bringing home some Scripture references dealing with the family. Please share them with each other.

Sincerely,

IMPROVING FAMILY TIES

Tell the children that building a stronger family is wise. Ask each child to choose a member of their family they would like to get to know better or to feel closer to. Give each child a copy of the following suggestions for the family member they choose.

PARENTS:
1. Volunteer to do a chore regularly. (Such as drying dishes, helping fold clothes, washing the car or cleaning the garage.)
2. Surprise them by doing some work around the house without being asked.
3. Watch a ball game with them and ask a few questions.
4. Ask them to tell you about things they did when they were your age.
5. Ask them to tell you about the work they do outside your home. Maybe you could visit where one, or both, of them work.
6. If you do not already do so, find a time to share Bible stories and pray together.

OLDER BROTHER OR SISTER:
1. Say something nice to him/her that you really mean.
2. Play a game with him/her and be a good sport about winning or losing.
3. Ask his/her advice about something and listen to the answer.
4. Do one of his/her chores as a surprise.

YOUNGER BROTHER OR SISTER:
1. Ask him/her to play a simple game with you.
2. Teach him/her a new skill, such as tying shoes, setting the table or braiding hair.
3. Offer to read him/her a storybook.
4. Ask him/her to tell you what some of his/her favorite things are.
5. Help him/her do a chore.

DEMONSTRATING LOVE AWAY FROM HOME

PUPPET TALKS

Many times children find it easier to express their true feelings through puppets rather than in face to face discussions. Mount the puppets found on page 58. Construct a simple puppet stage from chairs and blanket or cardboard box. Give one of the following situations, and let some of your children take it from there. You and the other children can be the audience. Remember, different children may play out the same situation differently. Give them a Scripture verse which they can use.

1. Wilma asks Grandma Wiseman how she should act toward her friend Susie whose parents are getting a divorce. "A friend loveth at all times . . . ." Proverbs 17:17
2. William is mad at his friend, Jacob, and has been tattling to the teacher about all the little things he thinks Jacob is doing wrong. Now he is beginning to feel sorry. "A talebearer revealeth secrets: but he that is of a faithful spirit concealeth the matter." Proverbs 11:13
3. Wilma's friend, Mandy, is not acting like a friend. Lately she seems to want to fight all the time. Wilma asks Grandpa Wiseman what to do. "A soft answer turneth away wrath: but grievous words stir up anger." Proverbs 15:1

MORE PUPPET TALK

Encourage the children to use the puppets to make up their own situations. Pay attention to what is being said. This is an activity that might reveal problems specifically bothering the children. Make note of topics that might need to be dealt with in the future.

BRAINSTORMING

Have the children quickly name things that give them problems outside the home. (Remember that many of today's children spend a great deal of time outside the home, not only at public school but at babysitters and day-care centers after school.) Often unique problems arise from these social situations.

"Hear, O my son, and receive my sayings; and the years of thy life shall be many." Proverbs 4:10

WISDOM AND HEALTH

Ask the children if they think caring for the bodies God gave them is wise. Let them discuss ways of caring for their bodies. Check the public library for books about health care for the age group you are working with.

WISDOM AND SAFETY

Discuss wisdom and safety rules with the children. Many law enforcement agencies offer booklets about safety for children. Some of these include coloring or activity pages.

WISE FRIENDS

"The wise in heart will receive commandments...."   Proverbs 10:8

(Grandma Wiseman)

(Grandpa Wiseman)

(Wilma Wiseman)

(William Wiseman)

WISE CREATIONS

Using the pattern given, cut a poster board owl for each child. Or, have someone cut them from thin plywood for you. The children can print Proverbs 14:1 on them. (If they are made of wood, they should be painted first.) Add a piece of strip magnet to the backside to make a decorative reminder of wisdom for mothers.

"Every wise woman buildeth her house..." Prov. 14:1

RECYCLED RICHES

Most people believe recycling material goods is wise. Bring a collection of egg cartons, empty juice cans, string, margarine tubs and lids, old greeting cards and other trash you can collect. Challenge the children to create something useful out of some of the items.

NEEDLECRAFT

Children are often capable of detailed needlecraft; and boys often seem as interested as girls. If you, a co-teacher or a class grandparent has a skill in one of these areas, why not let the children try it? This brief saying could be done with counted cross-stitch (large weave cloth and large needle), burlap and crewel yarn, or plastic canvas and yarn. The ends of the cloth can be raveled, making a frame unnecessary.

"GET WISDOM" PROVERBS 4:5

WISDOM IN SONG AND RHYME

"Wise men lay up knowledge...." Proverbs 10:14

SONGS

To the tune of "All Around the Mulberry Bush" teach the children the following words.

When I practice wi-s-dom,
I make each day go smoothly.
There's time for work and time for play,
When I practice wisdom.

These words are set to the tune of "The Farmer in the Dell."

Wisdom comes from God,
Wisdom comes from God,
So read your Bible—pray each day.
Wisdom comes from God.

Ask the children to think up additional verses using the two tunes above.

ACTION RHYMES
ANIMAL WISDOM

Ants are weak,
   (*Run fingers around like many ants.*)
But they work, work, work.
Rabbits are not strong,
   (*Hop like a bunny.*)
But their homes are hidden.
Locusts have no king,
   (*Have hands form crown.*)
But they cooperate.
The spider weaves her webs,
   (*Pretend to weave.*)
As God has bidden.

WISDOM

WISDOM IS:
Learning God's Word,
   (*Hold hands as open Bible.*)
Asking God's help,
   (*Fold hands in prayer.*)
Doing God's will.
   (*Walk around.*)

IN THE BIBLE
AN ACTION SONG
Words and Music by Muriel Larson

Where can we find the Words of God? In the Bible, In the Bible! Where can we find the truth and way? In the Bible, In the Bible! Where can we find God's promises? In the Bible, In the Bible! Where can we find answers each day? In God's Word, the Bi-ble!

At first, all the children may just shout "In the Bible" in response to the first three questions. At the same time, they can raise their Bibles or point to your raised Bible. Or, they can clap on the rests just before the answer and on every other beat of the last phrase.

After learning the song, the boys and girls may alternate in singing the questions and the answers, still raising their Bibles at the answer.

Or children can march around in a circle, stopping at the end of each question to clap and sing the answer.

In between singing, you might want to ask the children some questions:
1. The words of God are found in Scripture verses. Can anyone quote a Scripture verse?
2. Who called Himself "the truth and the way"?
3. Does anyone know a promise from the Bible?
4. How can God's Word make us strong?

WRITING ABOUT WISDOM

"If thou be wise, thou shalt be wise for thyself...." Proverbs 9:12

INTERVIEWS

Give the children a week to ask as many people as possible, "What do you think wisdom is?" Tell them to write down the answers they are given. The next week, allow time to share the responses the children received. Let them decide what they feel is the best answer.

TELL ABOUT....

"The wisest person I know is _____ _____, because...."

Give each child a piece of primary manuscript paper and let them complete the thought. Invite the children to share their writings, but do not force them to do so.

Here is another idea to be used in the same way, "Wisdom is important because...."

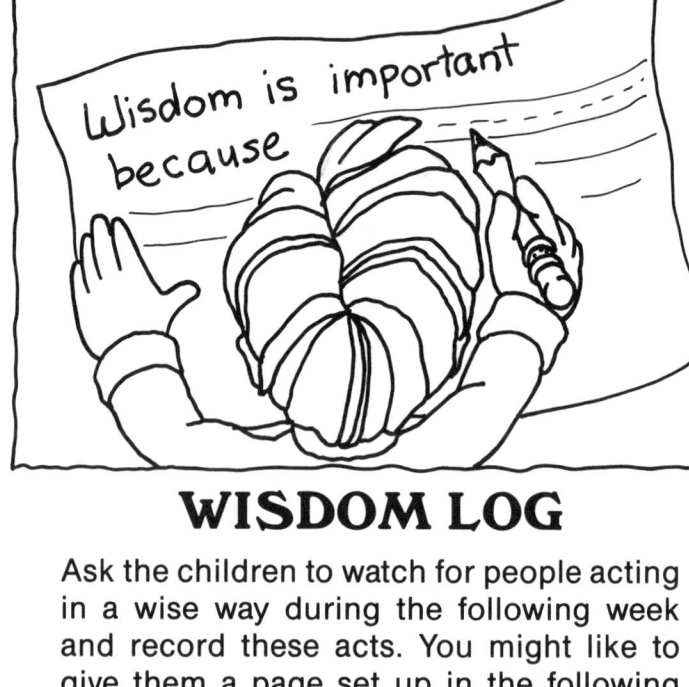

WISDOM LOG

Ask the children to watch for people acting in a wise way during the following week and record these acts. You might like to give them a page set up in the following manner to aid them.

DAY	TIME	PERSON	ACTION

GETTING TO KNOW WISDOM

Because many people have moved away from their hometowns, a lot of today's children do not have the advantage of a close, frequent relationship with their grandparents. Why not approach some of the wise, older Christians in your congregation about participating in this unit? Those who are healthy and able to be out might be willing to serve as "class grandparents" for a few sessions. Do not overlook shut-ins. If their health would not be put at risk and they are mentally alert, they might be blessed by a visit from a small group of your children.

Before beginning either experiment, talk to your children about the wisdom that comes from years of living as a Christian. Play a recording of Bill and Gloria Gaither's "The Longer I Serve Him", to help them understand this idea. Review rules of behavior and the respect due these older Christians.

CLASS GRANDPARENTS

Invite several older persons to come and work as class aides for several sessions. Encourage them to share the ways serving Jesus has blessed them.

CARRY-IN TEA PARTY

If you have several shut-ins who are healthy enough to have young visitors come, a carry-in tea party might be a special treat. Check with the shut-in and a family member to see if this can be arranged, and on food restrictions for the shut-in. Divide your children into small groups of three or four, plus an adult sponsor.

Plan a tea-party basket consisting of tea and hot chocolate, cookies or pound cake (you can purchase sugarless mixes if a shut-in is diabetic), cups, saucers and dessert plates.

If the person you are visiting has been a member of your congregation for a long time, ask him, or her, to tell the children about the early years of the church and what life was like at that time. (Our congregation is over one hundred years old, and one of our dear members who is over ninety, is a great source of church history. She delights youngsters with a tale of being stopped for speeding while driving a horse and buggy.)

Have your class present each of the "class grandparents" with a certificate.

WISDOM AWARD

To: _____

in honor and recognition of sharing with us
your wisdom which has come from years
of serving our Lord Jesus Christ.

From: _____

Shining Star Publications, Copyright © 1988, A division of Good Apple, Inc.

SS847

WISDOM TREASURE HUNT

"Happy is the man that findeth wisdom...." Proverbs 3:13

Children love treasure hunts. With a little advance planning, you can treat your class to a treasure hunt using the book of Proverbs as a guide. If your children are too young to look up the references, assign one adult (teacher or class grandparent) to each of the two groups. The treasure at the end of the hunt can be a sack of candy or some small items from a religious bookstore, such as bookmarks with a quote from Proverbs.

Give the captain of each group the first clue. Then tell the groups to proceed.

GROUP I
1. Look under the edge of the object mentioned in Proverbs 9:14.
2. Under the object mentioned in Proverbs 12:12 you will find another clue.
3. Feel around the edge of what is mentioned in Proverbs 7:6 for clue #3.
4. The treasure is guarded by what is mentioned in Proverbs 26:17. You may need to bring in a stuffed dog unless your classroom already has one. Have the dog casually sitting on the concealed treasure.

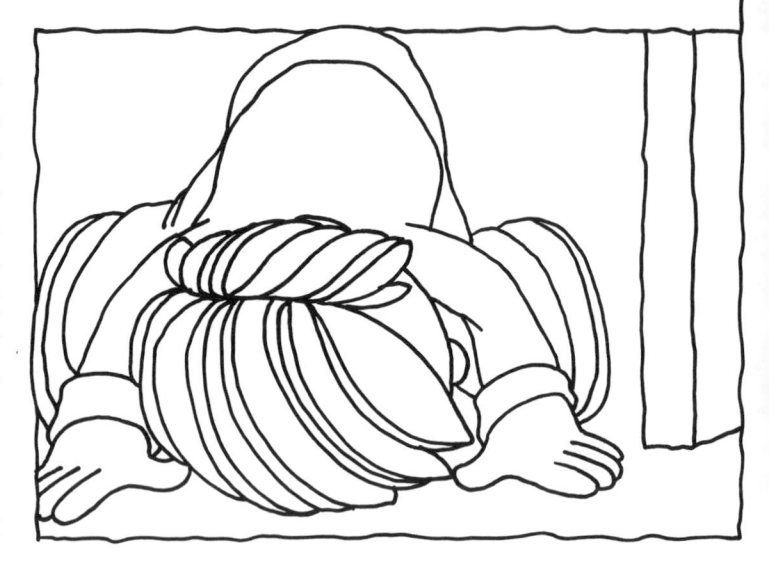

GROUP II
1. Under one of what is mentioned in Proverbs 27:18, you will find a clue.
2. Search what is found in Proverbs 7:16 for clue #2.
3. Instead of going in and out of what is mentioned in Proverbs 26:14, look carefully instead.
4. The treasure is guarded by what is mentioned in Proverbs 26:17.

Encourage the winners to share with the other group.

Remind the children that the true treasure in the game was the Word of God and the wisdom it gives us.

THE BIBLE TEACHES US HOW TO LISTEN

Noah is a good biblical example of the importance of LISTENING. Use the bulletin board, activities, song, crafts and games in this chapter to reinforce LISTENING skills.

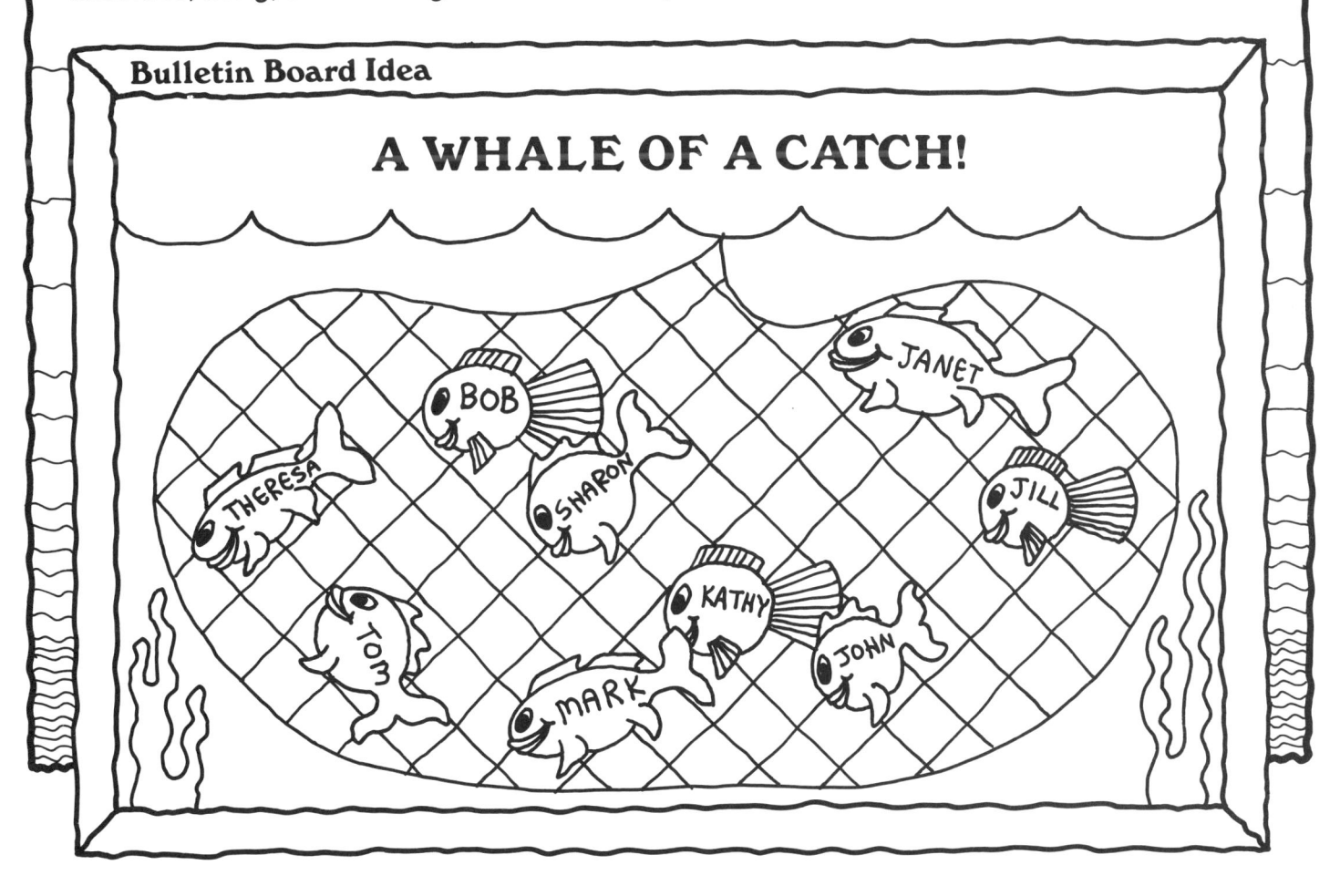

Bulletin Board Idea

A WHALE OF A CATCH!

PURPOSE: To give visual recognition to children for listening and following instructions, memorizing appropriate Scripture or changing classroom behavior, etc. Awarding children with a fish will depend on your immediate goals.

PROCEDURE:
1. Cover the bulletin board with blue-green paper. Use an overhead projector to enlarge waves and net onto bulletin board. Draw on details with a wide-tip marker. (Attach a piece of net to create a three-dimensional effect.)
2. Reproduce the fish patterns found on page 66, using different colors of construction paper.
3. Discuss the classroom goal—memorizing Scripture, behavior modification, etc. The children should understand what they must do to receive a fish. Each time a child memorizes a Bible verse, follows directions or accomplishes any prearranged goal, he gets to put his name on a fish and attach it to the bulletin board in the fisherman's net.
4. As a class, how fast can the children fill the net?

Shining Star Publications, Copyright © 1988, A division of Good Apple, Inc.

SS847

WHALE OF A CATCH PATTERNS

THE STORY OF JONAH

Jonah is a brief book with a fast-paced narrative. By dividing your class into four groups, with a parent or teacher in each group, the book can easily be read and condensed within a few minutes. Classes which contain mostly pre-readers or beginning readers can have the parent or teacher read the material. Encourage the children to retell the story to the class.

GROUP 1—CHAPTER 1

Since Chapter 1 is the beginning, this group will need no background.

QUESTIONS TO BE ANSWERED:
1. What did God tell Jonah to do? (1:2)
2. What did Jonah do? (1:3)
3. What happened to the ship Jonah was on? (1:4)
4. What did Jonah tell the men of the ship to do to him? (1:12)
5. Did they want to do it? (1:13, 14)
6. Did they? (1:15)
7. What happened when Jonah hit the water? (1:17)

GROUP 2—CHAPTER 2

Jonah was told by God to do something and did not obey. He found himself inside a big fish.

QUESTIONS TO BE ANSWERED:
1. What did Jonah do inside the fish? (2:1)
2. What did Jonah promise God? (2:9)
3. How did God answer Jonah's prayer? (2:10)

GROUP 3—CHAPTER 3

By the time we reach Chapter 3 Jonah has been swallowed by a big fish and spit out safely on dry land.

QUESTIONS TO BE ANSWERED:
1. What did God tell Jonah to do? (3:2)
2. What did Jonah do? (3:3)
3. Did the people of Nineveh pay any attention to him? (3:5)
4. What did they do? (3:6-9)
5. What did God do? (3:10)

GROUP 4—CHAPTER 4

After Jonah finally preached to the people of Nineveh, they repented, and God decided to let them live.

QUESTIONS TO BE ANSWERED:
1. Was Jonah happy that God decided not to destroy Nineveh and all its people? (4:1)
2. What did God use to try to teach Jonah a lesson? (4:6-9)
3. Do you think God loved the people of Nineveh? (4:10,11)

COMBINED GROUP QUESTIONS:
1. Was Jonah a good listener? Why or why not?
2. Were the people of Nineveh good listeners? What proof do you have?
3. Do you think Jonah loved the people of Nineveh?
4. Can you put the events of the story of Jonah in their proper order?

JONAH
Words and Music by Helen Friesen

God told Jo-nah, "Be my mess-en-ger; Nin-e-veh is wick-ed, they need to hear the Word.
Preach and tell them to re-pent to-day, I will send des-truc-tion, so now do not de-lay!"

Jo-nah chose to run a-way to sea, Got on board and thought how hap-py he would be;
When the sea got rough and winds did blow, Sail-ors woke up Jo-nah, "we're fright-ened, don't you know?"

Jo-nah knew he'd dis-o-beyed the Lord, "May-be I should let you throw me ov-er-board."
When the sail-ors did-n't dis-a-gree, They tossed Jo-nah in-to the aw-ful storm-y sea.

God pre-pared a whop-per of a fish; Did the fish think Jo-nah was a tast-y dish?
In the fish he stayed for three days more, Then the fish did spit him up-on the rock-y shore.

When the peo-ple heard what God had said, They re-pent-ed quick-ly put ash-es on their head.
An-gry Jo-nah said to God on high, "Let those peo-ple per-ish, they all de-serve to die."

Jo-nah sat out-side the cit-y wall, Wait-ed for the fire up-on them all to fall;
When God spared them from an aw-ful doom, Dis-ap-point-ed Jo-nah, he saw no fi-ery tomb.

FOLLOWING INSTRUCTIONS

Most games have one thing in common; the players must follow instructions. As children become older they learn to follow more complicated instructions.

After playing any of the following games, remind the children that the instructions God gave to Jonah were very simple. Jonah did not misunderstand God. Jonah did not obey the instructions he heard.

LISTEN, REMEMBER, DO

Depending on the age of your children, give a series of three to five simple instructions to each child. For example: Stand up, walk around the table, pick up the book on the table, sit down. Be certain everyone has a turn. If the children seem to be enjoying this activity, increase your list of instructions by one and continue. It is always best to stop an activity before interest dies, so be alert for signs of restlessness.

Another version of this game is to let everyone follow the same list of instructions at once. With a large group this may create chaos, but it is fun with a smaller number of children.

OBSTACLE COURSE

Using boxes with the bottoms cut out, piano benches, large blocks padded with blankets and other safe materials, create an obstacle course within your classroom. (A more elaborate version can be constructed outside, especially if playground equipment is available.) Be sure to keep all of the activities required within the ability of your most nonathletic child. Also look carefully at the children in your class. (It would be a disaster to have an overweight child not be able to get through an object.)

Explain the course to the children. Emphasize that the purpose of the activity is to complete all the activities in order, not necessarily with a great deal of speed. Either demonstrate your instructions or have an older child do the course first, as some younger children may still be having trouble with over, under, around and through. If a child forgets in the middle of the course, repeat the sequence for him. Compliment each child on trying to follow your instructions.

IT LOOKS FISHY

Cut several 4" fish from four colors of construction paper. (See patterns on page 66.) Tape them within 4" of each other in a mixed pattern. Make a cardboard spinner using the four colors. Let the children take turns putting right foot, left foot, right hand and left hand on color indicated by the spinner.

RIDDLES, RHYMES AND REASONING

Children love riddles, and riddles are good starters for the thought process. Give one or two riddles and challenge children to make up their own riddles about the story of Jonah.

Example:
What can be peaceful to some, but stormy and cold to a prophet who did not do what he was told? Answer: SEA

FINGERPLAY

There was a man named Jonah
(*Hold right index finger up.*)
For whom God had a plan.
"Go preach My Word in Nineveh."
But Jonah the other way ran.
(*Make "Jonah" run away.*)

There came a fish in the ocean
(*Make left hand swim like a fish.*)
Which God made with a plan
To make the disobedient Jonah
Again become God's man.

The fish and Jonah got together.
(*Have "fish" swallow "Jonah".*)
It was all a part of God's plan.
And when God spoke the next time,
Jonah listened to His command.
(*Have "Jonah" stand at attention.*)

LISTEN

When God speaks,
(*Hold hand to ear.*)
I'll listen and do
(*Point to self.*)
All of the things
He tells me to.

God speaks through
His Word to us today.
(*Hold hands as Bible.*)
It is right for us
to listen and obey.

WHAT IF?

What do you think would have happened if . . .
1. Jonah had listened to God the first time?
2. The men on the ship had not agreed to throw Jonah overboard?
3. God had not prepared the big fish?
4. Jonah had really loved the people of Nineveh?

FISH CRAFTS
NET BANNER

Cut a piece of net 8" x 10" for each child from a potato or citrus fruit sack. Cut the letters "LISTEN TO GOD" from 1" pieces of felt. Let the children glue the pieces into place. Weave dowel rods 12" x ¼" into the top. The children may choose to add a felt Jonah, or fish, to their banner. (See page 66 for fish patterns.)

FISH PILLOW

Using the fish patterns on page 66, cut two cloth fish for each child. Putting the right sides together, show the children how to sew a simple running stitch. Encourage them to keep their stitches small. Help them with knots and endings. Demonstrate how to clip seams and turn the pillow right side out, stuff and close.

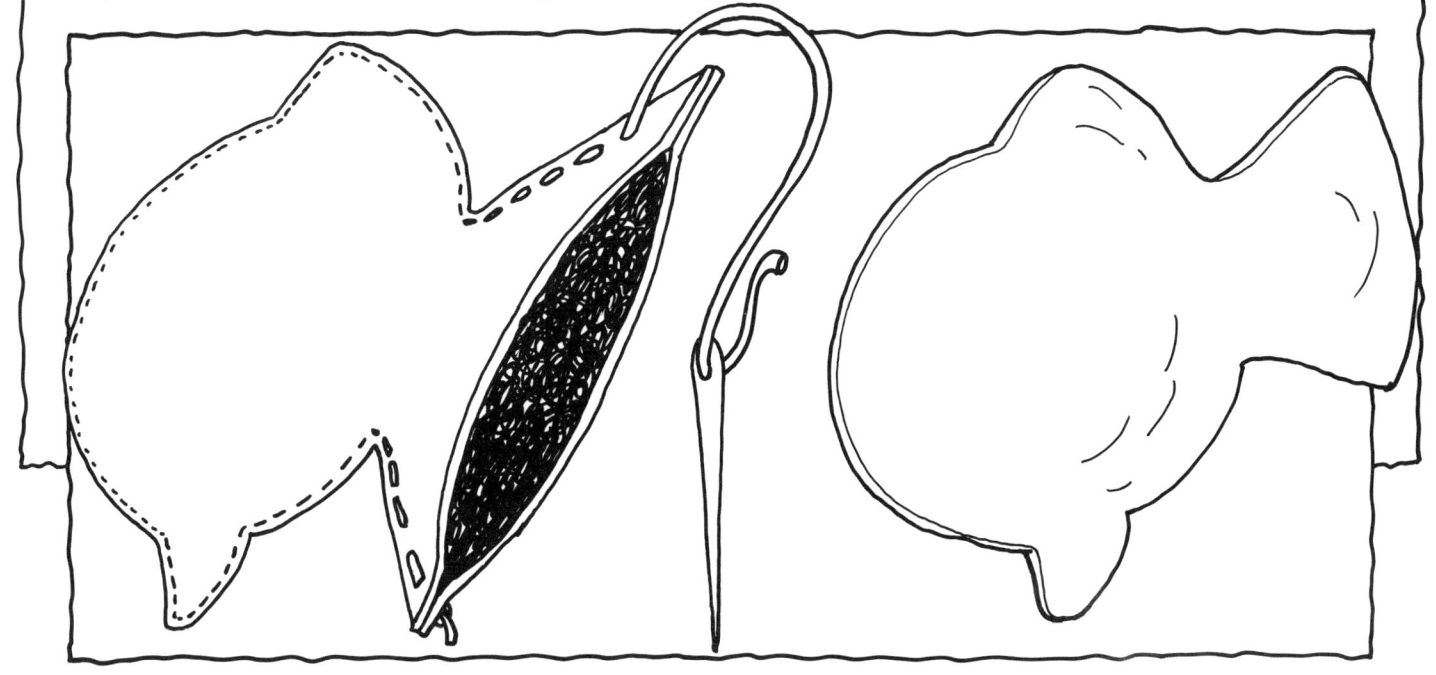

JONAH ACTIVITIES

Your children should now realize that Jonah's trouble came from not obeying God's command. Encourage them to transfer that knowledge into present day situations with the activities on this page.

JONAH'S JOURNAL

Encourage the children to pretend that they are Jonah stranded in the belly of the whale for three days. Have each child write a journal during the three days, recording actions and feelings.

SCRIPTURAL TWIST

Have the children rewrite the story of Jonah pretending to be the whale instead of Jonah. How did the whale feel to have a man moving around inside him for three days? Guide the stories by asking some questions: Did God give you a special job? Were you an important instrument in leading Jonah to God? How did you accomplish this task?

PUPPET PLAY

Provide three or four puppets for each group (three or four children), and let them write a play based on the above Scripture.

PEOPLE PLAY

Using the same Scripture as a base, encourage individuals to write a brief play to be presented by their classmates. After hearing these the group may decide to perform one or two of the plays.

In either of the above cases, if your class is made up of mostly younger children, you might let them decide upon a situation and role-play it instead of writing it out.

COMPLETE THE THOUGHT

Read Matthew 28:18-20 to the children and give them a sheet of primary manuscript paper on which you have written, "I do not want to be like Jonah so I will . . . ." Let each child complete the thought.

Shining Star Publications, Copyright © 1988, A division of Good Apple, Inc. SS847

PUZZLE PAGE

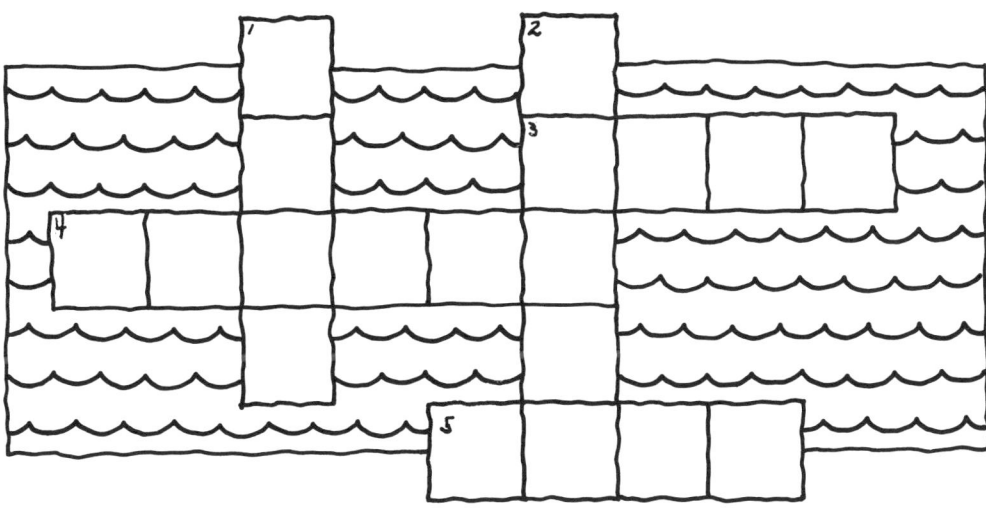

DOWN:
1. What God prepared to teach Jonah a lesson.
2. A man who did not listen to God.

ACROSS:
3. What Jonah learned to do.
4. When God's Word is spoken we should . . . .
5. What Jonah tried to use to run away from God.

WHAT IS IT?

Color the starred spaces gray and the dotted spaces blue.

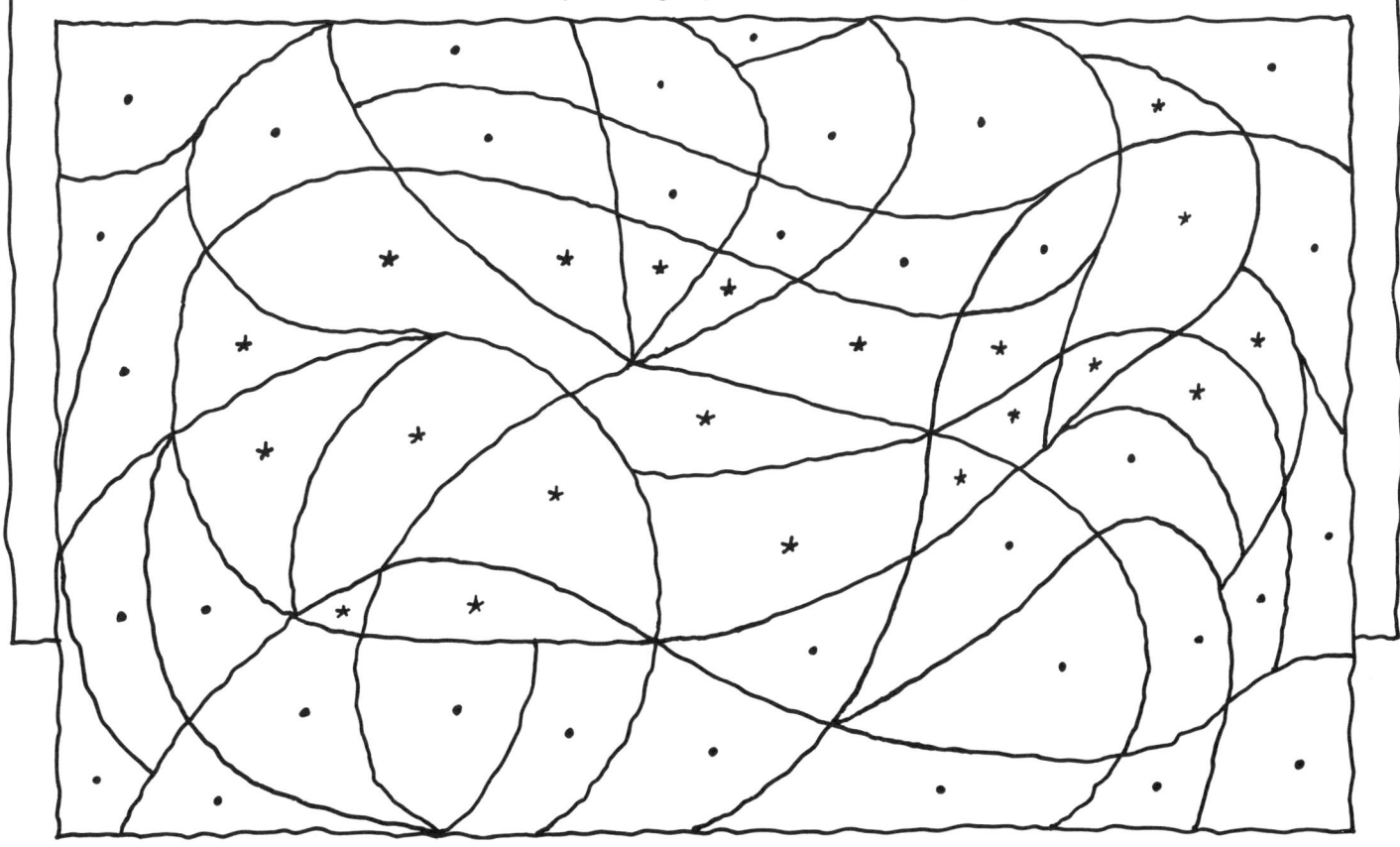

OTHER BIBLE PEOPLE WHO DID NOT LISTEN

Let the children discover that Jonah was not the only person recorded in the Bible who got into trouble by ignoring God's instructions.

MOSES
1. What did God tell Moses to do?
2. What did Moses do?
3. Why was that wrong?
4. What happened because of what Moses did?

NUMBERS 20:1-12

SAMSON
1. What was Samson never to let happen to his hair?
2. How did Samson let his hair be cut?
3. What happened because of this?

JUDGES 16:15-20

RICH YOUNG RULER
1. What did the young man ask Jesus to tell him about?
2. What did Jesus tell him to do?
3. Did the young man agree to do it?
4. How did the young man feel?

LUKE 18:18-23

PETER
1. What did Jesus warn Peter that Peter was about to do?
2. Did Peter think that he would do what Jesus prophesied?
3. Did Peter do what Jesus warned him about?

MATTHEW 26:33-35, 69-75

LET'S GO FISHIN'

If you have the courage, manpower and facilities, why not take your group fishing. If not, plan a party around a fishing theme. Many details will be the same.

FISHING TRIP

The key to this outing is safety. Make sure the location of your outing is as safe as possible (no rotting docks, for example) and that you have at least one adult for every two children. Stress to your adults that no child is to be left alone at any time. Many children today have never had the opportunity to go fishing, so, if all the necessary details can be worked out, this outing is worth the trouble.

Check local fishing laws! Your children probably will not need licenses, but your adults may.

FISHING PARTY

Make a fishing pond out of a child's swimming pool or other watertight container. Seal a red or blue construction paper fish, a balloon and a paper clip or other lightweight metal object inside a sealable sandwich bag. Upon arriving let each child fish with a pole equipped with a magnet. The children are to wear the fish caught to indicate which team they are on.

After pinning on the fish tag, the child is to blow up a balloon and add it to the team's catch in separate trash bags. Teachers may help with tying the balloons.

KEEPING YOUR CATCH

After all the children have arrived, divide the group into two teams. Tie a balloon to each child's ankle. The two teams will then try to break as many of the other team's balloons as possible within a two-minute period. The team with the most balloons left will be declared the team with the biggest catch.

DIGGING FOR WORMS

Tie candy worms in sandwich bags and hide the individual pieces in a haystack secured for this purpose. At a given signal let the children attack the stack and find as many "worms" as possible. (Be sure to show them an example of what they are looking for.)

SLIPPERY FISH

Line the two teams up facing each other. Have several water balloons ready. Using one, let the teams begin throwing it back and forth down the line. As the balloon breaks replace it with another.

FOOD

Fish sticks served with hush puppies (see recipe) and slaw will be easier than a real fish fry.

Hush puppies: Two cups of corn meal, 1 teaspoon of baking powder, ¼ teaspoon salt, an egg, some chopped onion and enough water to make a medium batter. Dropped by the spoonful and fried in hot oil, these will make a good treat to go with fish.

DEVOTIONAL

Bring along a fishing pole, bait, life jacket and any other equipment you feel might interest the children. Discuss the rules for safe and successful fishing.

Remind the children that Jonah forgot one of life's most important rules—a person should always listen to God.

STOP, LOOK AND LISTEN

Let the children make up some traffic signs to illustrate instructions give in God's Word. Some Scriptures to use as a basis for this activity might be: Mark 12:30; Acts 10:48; Ephesians 6:2; I Thessalonians 4:9; I Thessalonians 4:11; I John 3:11; I John 4:21.

Show the children the following signs or bring a driver's manual from your local Driver's License Facility.

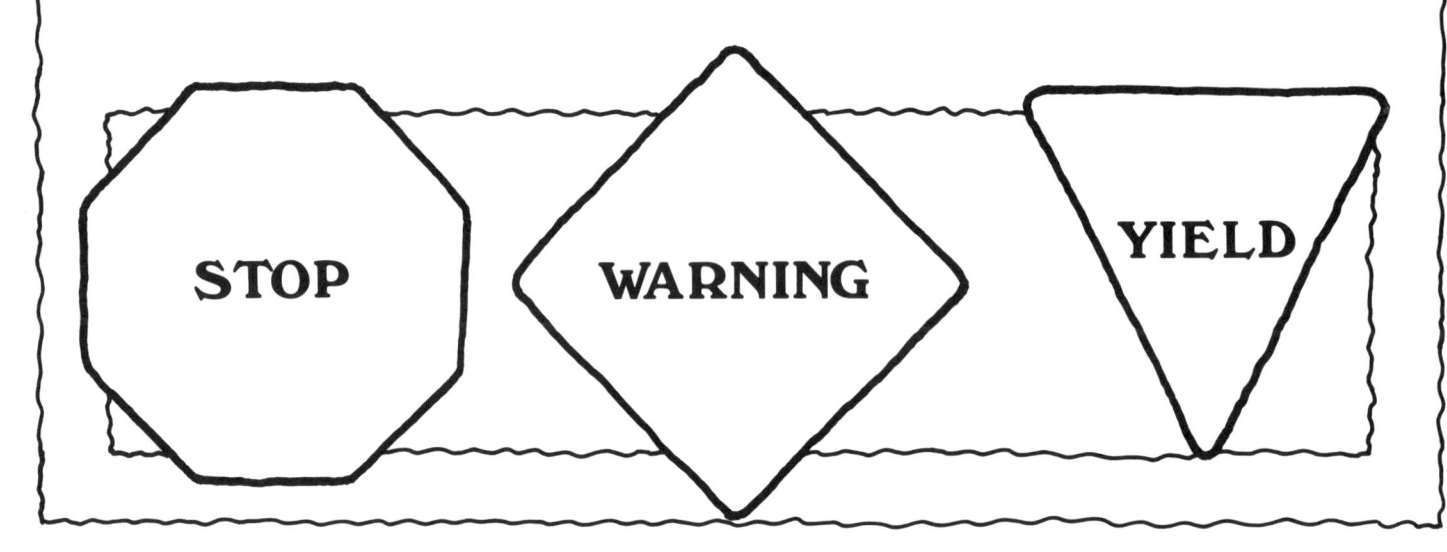

STOP **WARNING** **YIELD**

STOP! LOOK! AND LISTEN!
by
Phyllis C. Michael

(sheet music)

Before you say that unkind word, (1) STOP! (2) LOOK! and (3) LIS-TEN! Before you do that unkind deed, (1) STOP! (2) LOOK! and (3) LIS-TEN!

1. What, oh, what would you have done If you had been the other one?
2. What, oh, what would Jesus do If He were someone just like you?

What, oh, what can you do now To make things turn out right somehow?
Let Him help you do and say The kindest thing the kindest way.

Before you say that unkind word, (1) STOP! (2) LOOK! and (3) LIS-TEN! Before you do that unkind deed, (1) STOP! (2) LOOK! and (3) LIS-TEN.

THE BIBLE TEACHES US HOW TO FOLLOW

John the Baptist was a perfect example of a leader that knew how to follow. While teaching and leading the people, John often spoke of one greater than he—coming to save the world. Help your children learn how to follow as they learn the details of the life of John the Baptist, cousin of Jesus.

Bulletin Board Idea

Who was John's father? Zecharias
What was John's father's job? priest

WHO WAS JOHN?

PURPOSE: To help boys and girls become familiar with John the Baptist.

PROCEDURE:
1. Cover bulletin board with yellow paper.
2. Use an overhead projector to enlarge the figure of John and draw on background paper or cut out and mount on bulletin board. Cut 13 question marks from red paper and print a question, found on page 78, on each one. Cut out 13 large red circles and print the answer to one of the thirteen questions on each one.
3. After hearing the account of John in Luke 1:5-25 and 57-80 (see directions for sharing story and questions on page 78), review the material by randomly passing out the red circles with answers and let the children place them under the appropriate question mark on the bulletin board.

WHO WAS THIS MAN JOHN?

Often the background of John is skimmed over as we race toward the Christmas story. Give each child in your group (or divide into smaller groups) a question and ask them to listen for the answer. Read the account from Luke 1:5-25 and 57-80. After reading the Scripture as a group, if any of the children are uncertain about the answer to their questions, help them look up the specific Scripture beside the question. (You can give these to the children orally or write them on large construction paper question marks and pass them out.)

1. Who was John's father? Luke 1:5
2. What was John's father's job? Luke 1:5
3. Who was John's mother? Luke 1:5
4. Were they young or old? Luke 1:7
5. How many children did John's mother and father have? Luke 1:7
6. Who did Zacharias meet in the temple? Luke 1:11
7. What was Zacharias told? Luke 1:13
8. What was the child forbidden to drink? Luke 1:15
9. How did the angel prove to Zacharias that everything he said would happen? Luke 1:20
10. When John was born, what did the people want to name him? Luke 1:59
11. When did Zacharias get his speech back? Luke 1:63, 64
12. What did Zacharias prophesy John would do? Luke 1:76, 77
13. What do we know about John's childhood? Luke 1:80

After all the children feel confident about their answers, let them share with the entire group.

You might like to finish with some discussion questions.

1. Since John was the son of a priest, do you think he knew much about the Jewish religion? Why?
2. Since John's parents were old when he was born, do you think it is possible that someone else might have reared him for a part of his childhood? Who do you think that might have been?
3. Do you think Zacharias and Elizabeth probably told John about the strange circumstances of his birth?
4. Since Elizabeth and Mary were related, do you think John and Jesus might have met when they were children?

THE SPIRIT AND POWER OF ELIJAH

"And he shall go before him in the spirit and power of Elias . . . ." Luke 1:17

Trace the figures of John and Elijah on construction paper or poster board. Let the children list the likenesses on both figures.

Read about Elijah in II Kings 1:8-16.

Read to the children what Jesus had to say about John the Baptist. (Matthew 11:4-15)

Wore camel's hair clothing.

Ate locusts and wild honey.

Did not put needs above duty.

Wore girdle of leather.

Fed by ravens.

Preaching was direct and powerful.

Pointed out sin and need for repentance.

Prophecy was direct and powerful.

WILDERNESS LIFE

"... The voice of one crying in the wilderness . . . ."   Luke 3:4

Using maps, globes, Bible encyclopedia, Bible dictionaries, etc., lead the children in studying the area where John did his preaching. Topics to look up: desert, wilderness, animals of the Bible, John the Baptist.

GEOGRAPHY:
1. Locate: Jericho, Jerusalem, Bethlehem, Hebron. Approximately how far were each of these from the area where John preached?
2. Locate: Dead Sea, Mt. Nebo, Jordan River.
3. What was the climate like?
4. What type of vegetation and landscape would John have seen as he traveled around?
5. Can you locate this area on a present day map or globe?
6. How has this area changed? (You may need to borrow a present day geography book to get current information.)

BIOLOGY:
1. What types of animals might John have seen living in this area?
2. What are the needs and habits of these animals?
3. Draw pictures of some of the animals.

Encourage the children to watch the newspapers and newsmagazines for pictures of this area today. Mount these as they are brought to class.

MAP
Let the children sketch this simple map on the chalkboard or on shelf paper to use as a reference.

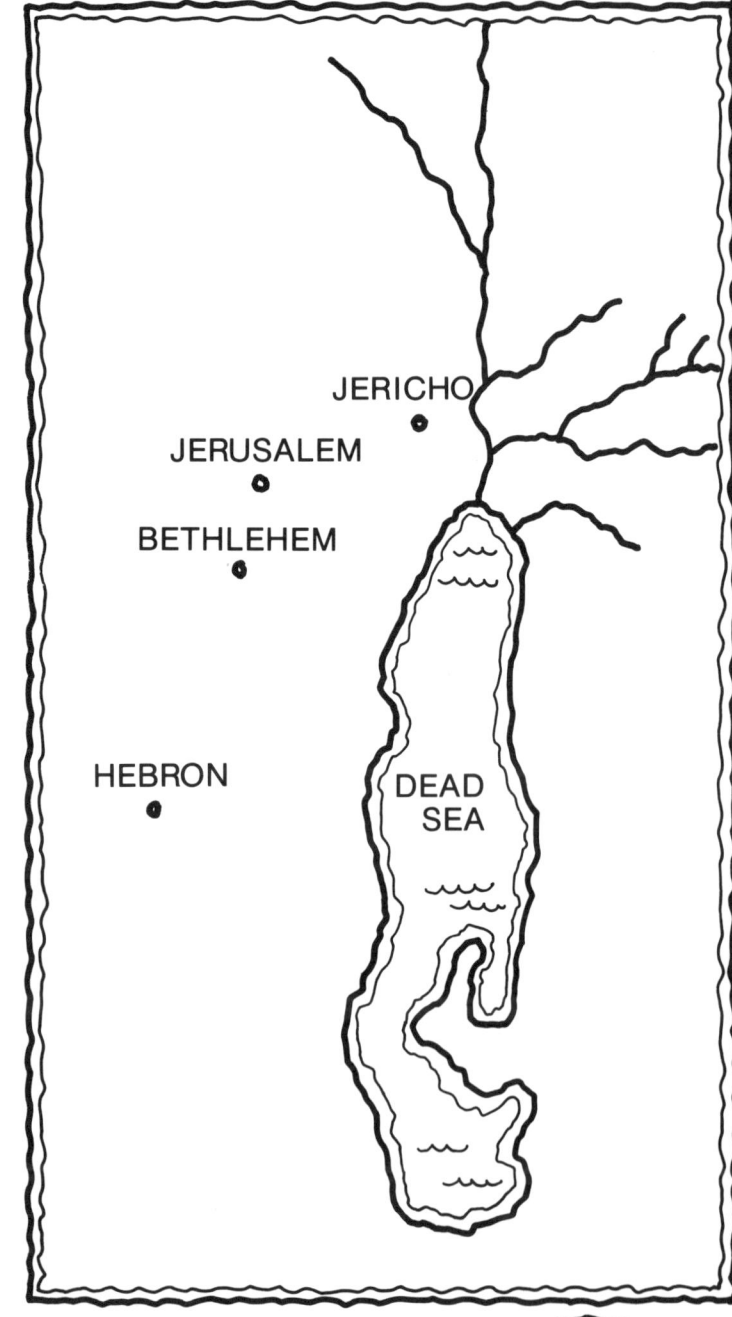

ART PROJECT

Using the information gathered from their studies of the area where John ministered, let the children construct a diorama of the area in which John's ministry took place.

GROUP WORK

If you decide to work as one large, or several small groups, you may want to construct your scene on a table top or inside a large carton.

Supplies: fabric, sand or sand paper, artificial grass scraps (or outdoor carpet scraps) tree branches, rocks, glue, paint, scissors, newspapers and construction paper. Let the children use their imaginations in planning the project. If you plan to make this a long term project, let them help gather supplies.

1. Land Construction: This group will build the basic background. They may want to use a papier-mâché base or other means to give the impression of depth and height. Paints and other coverings can then be used to make the scene more realistic.
2. Animals: Papier-mâché animals of the area made to scale with the background would add greatly to the scene.
3. People: If the scale will allow, "fashion" dolls could be dressed to represent John and the people who came to hear him. The dolls probably could be borrowed for the few weeks the project would be under construction and on display. Garage sales are another good source of these and are a good investment. They can be dressed as many different characters and used in other Bible-based units.

INDIVIDUAL WORK

Have each child bring a shoebox. Provide the same supplies listed for the group project. Let each child create his own scene. Instead of fashion dolls, people could be made from craft sticks or chenille wire.

Shining Star Publications, Copyright © 1988, A division of Good Apple, Inc.   SS847

VOICE CHOIR

Help your children learn a large block of Scripture by forming a voice choir. Even though not all children will say all verses, most will learn the entire block because of repetition.

GIRLS: In those days came John the Baptist, preaching in the wilderness of Judaea. And saying,

JOHN: Repent ye: for the kingdom of heaven is at hand.

GIRL: For this is he that was spoken of by the prophet Esaias, saying,

BOYS: The voice of one crying in the wilderness, Prepare ye the way of the Lord, make his paths straight.

GIRLS: And the same John had his raiment of camel's hair, and a leathern girdle about his loins; and his meat was locusts and wild honey.

BOYS: Then went out to him Jerusalem, and all Judaea, and all the region about Jordan, And were baptized of him in Jordan, confessing their sins.

GIRLS: But when he saw many of the Pharisees and Sadducees come to his baptism, he said unto them,

JOHN: O generation of vipers, who hath warned you to flee from the wrath to come? Bring forth therefore fruits meet for repentance: And think not to say within yourselves, We have Abraham to our father: for I say unto you, that God is able of these stones to raise up children unto Abraham. And now also the axe is laid unto the root of the trees: therefore every tree which bringeth not forth good fruit is hewn down, and cast into the fire. I indeed baptize you with water unto repentance: but he that cometh after me is mightier than I, whose shoes I am not worthy to bear: he shall baptize you with the Holy Ghost, and with fire: Whose fan is in his hand, and he will thoroughly purge his floor, and gather his wheat into the garner; but he will burn up the chaff with unquenchable fire.

BOYS: Then cometh Jesus from Galilee to Jordan unto John, to be baptized of him. But John forbad him, saying,

JOHN: I have need to be baptized of thee, and comest thou to me?

GIRLS: And Jesus answering said unto him,

BOYS: Suffer it to be so now: for thus it becometh us to fulfil all righteousness. Then he suffered him.

GIRLS: And Jesus, when he was baptized, went up straightway out of the water: and, lo, the heavens were opened unto him, and he saw the Spirit of God descending like a dove, and lighting upon him:

BOYS: And lo a voice from heaven, saying,

ALL: This is my beloved Son, in whom I am well pleased.

Matthew 3

(Reproduce and highlight each child's part.)

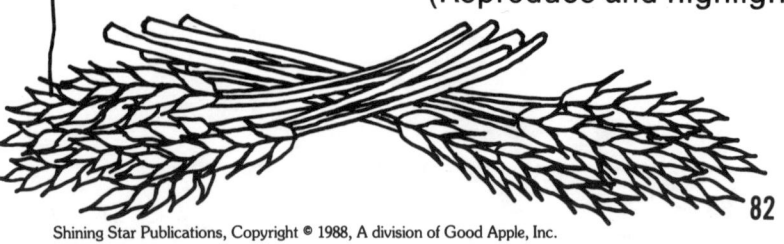

ATTITUDES

HE MEANT

Working as individuals or as small groups let the children describe what they think John meant by the following statements:

". . . but one mightier than I cometh, the latchet of whose shoes I am not worthy to unloose . . . ."   Luke 3:16

"He must increase, but I must decrease."   John 3:30

Ask the children to write down one attitude they think would describe John. Either have the children share what they have written, or collect the papers and read the ideas. Discuss the different ideas.

ACROSTIC

Challenge the children each to write an acrostic using John's name. Mount these on construction paper or poster board for display.

A FRIEND LIKE JOHN

Ask the children if they think John had the qualities of a good friend to Jesus? They will probably agree that he did.

Give each child an index card. Encourage them to write down the name of a person they would like to be a better friend to. Ask them to list three ways they will try to accomplish this.

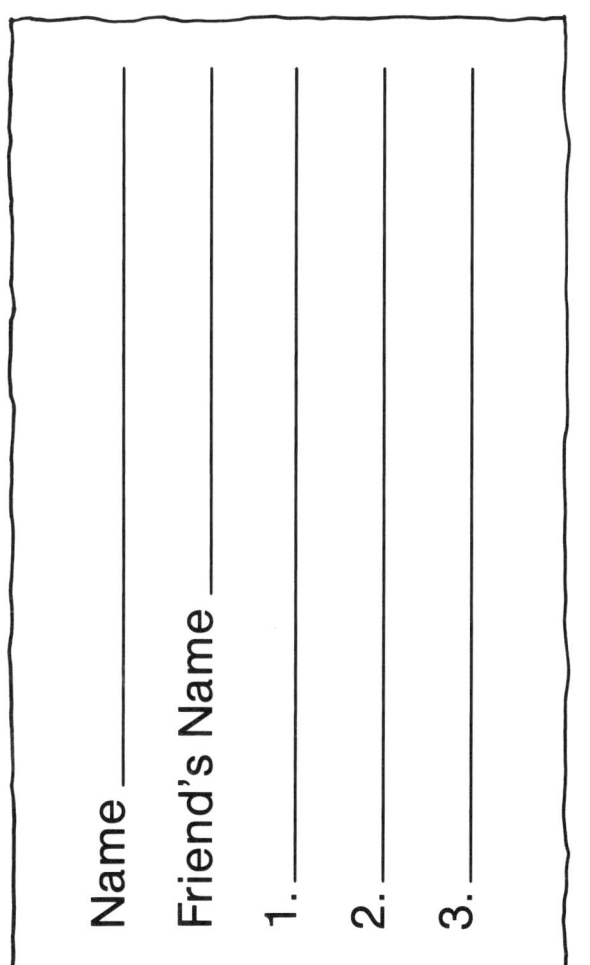

CAMEL'S HAIR WEAVING

Make a loom from cardboard using the pattern below. Find rough yarn for the children to use in weaving. The end result could be mats or a rough garment made by stitching two mats together. The purpose is for the children to feel the roughness of the materials. Emphasize that the camel's hair clothing worn by John would have been even rougher than what they are feeling (unless you have obtained true camel's hair yarn). Encourage the children to discuss how comfortable they think it would have been. Have various fabrics and yarns available for them to feel. Ask them why they think John wore this type of clothing.

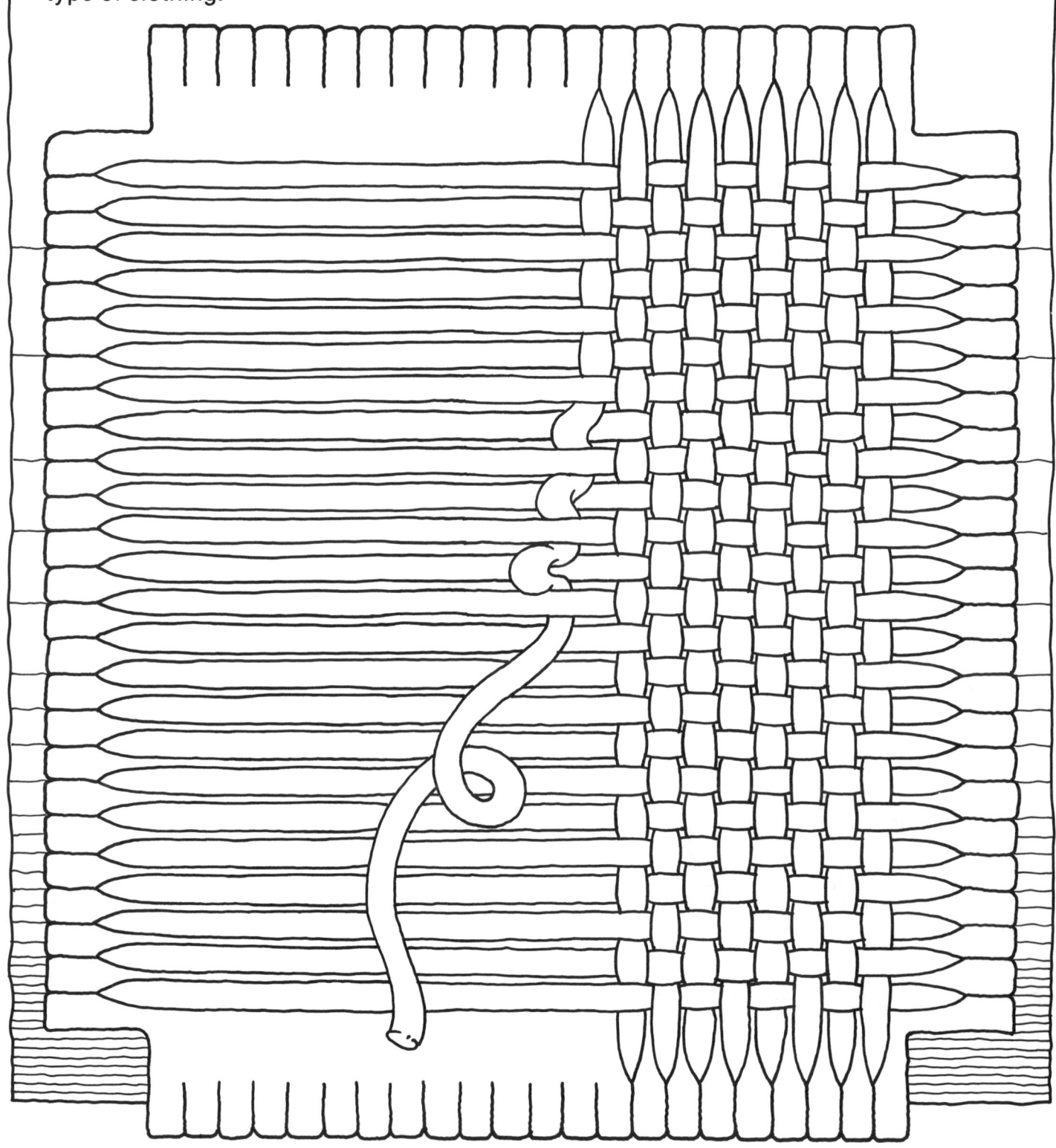

COLORING PAGE

85

LOCUSTS AND WILD HONEY

"... and his meat was locusts and wild honey."   Matthew 3:4

Locusts are said to taste like shrimp. You might let the children taste boiled or roasted shrimp to give them an idea of the flavor.

The honey you buy in the grocery store is not wild honey, but the idea will be the same. Honey can be tasted plain or used as a substitute for sugar in many recipes. The children probably will enjoy experimenting in the kitchen with some of the following recipes:

CORN BREAD

1½ cups corn meal
½ cup flour
½ teaspoon salt
1 teaspoon baking powder
2 tablespoons honey
1 egg, beaten
enough water to make a medium batter

Mix and pour into hot, greased pan. Bake in 350° oven for 20-30 minutes.

HONEY COOKIES

1 cup honey
1 cup margarine
1 egg
2 teaspoons vanilla
2 cups flour
1 teaspoon cinnamon
¼ teaspoon salt

Cream margarine. Add honey, egg and vanilla. Beat. Add flour, cinnamon and salt mixture. Drop by teaspoons on greased cookie sheet. Bake 10-13 minutes at 375°.

HONEY CRUNCH BALLS

Equal amounts of:
honey
crunchy peanut butter
powdered milk
coconut

Mix all ingredients together. If mixture is too thin, add more powdered milk. Make into balls and roll in extra coconut or crushed nuts. Store in refrigerator.

Shining Star Publications, Copyright © 1988, A division of Good Apple, Inc.   SS847

THE ORDER OF JOHN'S LIFE

Reproduce a copy of this page for each child. Have the children cut out the sections and place them in order. They can be glued to a piece of construction paper or made into a booklet.

A. Preaching

B. Baptism of Jesus

C. Imprisoned

D. Angel and Zacharias

E. Naming of Baby

F. Burial

WILDERNESS WANDERINGS

The area in which you live will determine how much "wilderness" is available to you. It may be a back pasture of a farm, a state or city park, the church property or a leader's backyard. Just being out of doors will lend specialness to this outing. It will make the children better able to identify with John who spent so much time in the wilderness. Plan a camp out, if at all possible. If this is not safe because of location, lack of equipment or other reasons, plan a cookout after dark.

GROUPING

Divide the children into small groups of travelers according to the number of children present. Give them cards marked Jerusalem, Bethlehem, Jericho or Hebron. These cards can be used to group children for games or chores.

TRAVELING TO THE JORDAN

Assign each group an adult leader who will lead them on a nature hike (each in a different direction). Tell the leaders to try and arrive back at the camp site approximately the same time. In this way the children can sense the excitement of travelers reaching a joint destination.

MAKING CAMP

Give each group chores to get the campsite ready. These might include getting water, gathering firewood (check local laws), unrolling bedding. Try to have tents set up before the children arrive. Suggest to the children that many people who went out to hear John may have camped in the area before returning home.

GATHERING LOCUSTS AND WILD HONEY

Hide food provisions in a safe place before the children arrive. It would be a good idea to keep a list of what was hidden and where. Hot dog buns will do you little good if you cannot find the hot dogs. (Frozen hot dogs which are well sealed can be hidden for a short time.)

Check all packages when they are returned to the cook to be sure they have not been damaged by a wild animal. Do not use anything that might be contaminated.

Tell the children that John seems to have eaten whatever was available in the area where he was preaching. Give them the boundaries where the food is hidden and let them begin their search.

CAMPFIRE

Before going to bed or going home, gather the children around the campfire. Let them share what they have learned about John. If they have learned the voice choir by memory, it would be a beautiful way to close this session.

Keep the session quiet so the children can feel the closeness to God which being out of doors provides.

A quiet outdoor setting will help the children feel the nearness of God.

WAKE UP

Allow time for individual quiet time before breakfast. Be sure leaders set the example in this, instead of using the time to prepare breakfast. (Spiritual food is more important then physical food at this time.)

THE BIBLE TEACHES US HOW TO BE HAPPY

BLESSED ARE

- THE POOR IN SPIRIT
- THEY THAT MOURN
- THE MEEK
- THOSE THAT HUNGER AND THIRST AFTER RIGHTEOUSNESS
- THE MERCIFUL
- THE PURE IN HEART
- THE PEACEMAKERS
- THE PERSECUTED

PURPOSE: To keep the main thoughts of the beatitudes before the children in a happy setting.

PROCEDURE:
1. Make the background sky blue.
2. Clouds can be made of a thin layer of cotton glued to the background. Glue letters onto clouds.
3. Strips of the rainbow should be cut from eight colors (or shades such as violet and purple) of construction paper or poster board. Lettering can be done with markers.
4. Small clouds will make an attractive border.

Shining Star Publications, Copyright © 1988, A division of Good Apple, Inc.

SS847

THE BEATITUDES
Music By
Helen Friesen

Blessed are the poor in spirit: for theirs is the kingdom of heaven. Blessed are they that mourn: for they shall be comforted. Blessed are the meek: for they shall inherit the earth. Blessed are they which do hunger and thirst, thirst after righteousness: for they shall be filled, they shall be filled. Blessed are the merciful: for they shall obtain mercy. Blessed are the pure in heart: for they shall see God. Blessed are the peacemakers: for they shall be called children of God. Blessed are they which are persecuted for righteousness' sake: for theirs is the kingdom of heaven. Blessed are ye, when men shall revile you, and persecute you, and shall say all manner of evil against you falsely, for my sake. Rejoice, and be exceeding glad: for great is your reward in heaven.

Shining Star Publications, Copyright © 1988, A division of Good Apple, Inc.

JESUS PUPPET

"... and when he was set, his disciples came unto him ...." Matthew 5:1

Reproduce these for each child. Mount the stick for the Jesus puppet to the top portion only. By folding along the dotted lines, the puppet can be made to sit.

Make a base for these puppets by cutting the top and bottom rings from a six-ounce juice can, cutting it in half and making two small slits.

These puppets can be used in helping the children to learn the beatitudes. They could also be used to illustrate the song found on the previous page.

Shining Star Publications, Copyright © 1988, A division of Good Apple, Inc. SS847

TRUE SUCCESS

"Blessed are the poor in spirit: for theirs is the kingdom of heaven."   Matthew 5:3

A long running commercial stressed that people "never outgrow their need for" a certain product. Children and even teenagers often feel that when they grow up they will not need to depend on anyone. Lead them through a Bible search to show them how a person should grow to depend more and more on God.

Cut pictures of people from magazines who fit the present day image of success. Paste these onto construction paper and trim around the picture. On the back of each print one of the Scripture references found on this page.

Give each of the children one of the "paper dolls" and ask them to look up the Scripture and share it with the class. Have the children discuss how that Scripture might apply to a person like the one pictured. Stress the fact that only those who realize they have a need for God in their lives are truly successful.

". . . the Lord is the strength of my life . . . ."   Psalm 27:1

"It is better to trust in the Lord than to put confidence in man."   Psalm 118:8

"Some trust in chariots, and some in horses: but we will remember the name of the Lord our God."   Psalm 20:7

". . . when I am weak, then am I strong."   II Corinthians 12:10

". . . Blessed are all they that put their trust in him."   Psalm 2:12

". . . without thy mind would I do nothing . . . ."   Philemon 1:14

"Thou wilt keep him in perfect peace, whose mind is stayed on thee . . . ."   Isaiah 26:3

"Cast thy burden upon the Lord, and he shall sustain thee . . . ."   Psalm 55:22

". . . Increase our faith."   Luke 17:5

". . . the Lord shall be thy confidence, and shall keep thy foot from being taken."   Proverbs 3:26

Shining Star Publications, Copyright © 1988, A division of Good Apple, Inc.   SS847

CONSTRUCTIVE MOURNING

"Blessed are they that mourn: for they shall be comforted." Matthew 5:4

Lead the children in discovering that to mourn or to express sorrow for sin can be the beginning of recovery, whether it is sins that mar our world, sins of friends or our own.

Tape a large sheet of paper on the wall and title it, "Things About Which We Mourn." Let the children cut headlines from newspapers or pictures from magazines showing sins, or the results of sins, that are in our world.

Discuss things Christians can do to make the world a better place.

One way the children may decide to help is to pray about these things. Suggest that prayer is also an effective means of dealing with sin in the lives of those we care about, as well as our own lives.

Let them make prayer reminder bookmarks to keep in their Bibles. These can be made of poster board and yarn.

Encourage the children to write "letters to God" in which they confess to Him sin in their lives. These could be kept in the form of a journal or torn up after written.

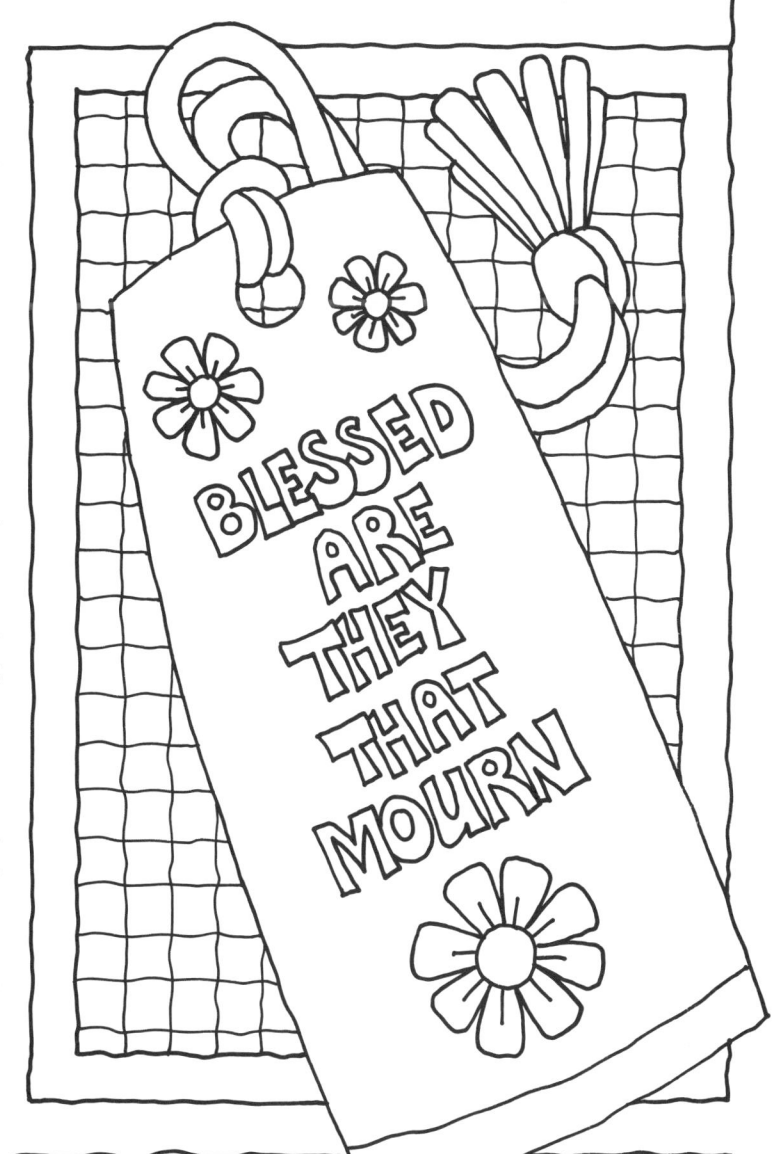

Shining Star Publications, Copyright © 1988, A division of Good Apple, Inc.   SS847

THE MEEKNESS MINUTES

"Blessed are the meek: for they shall inherit the earth."   Matthew 5:5

The common concept of meekness is weakness. This is totally false, and unattractive to today's young people. Meekness, in reality, is strength that has been placed voluntarily in the control of another—in the case of a Christian, control by the Lord.

After brainstorming, let your group choose from one of the five creative writing ideas. Gather the results and arrange in newspaper form. Distribute at your next gathering or mail to each class member.

BRAINSTORM

In a three-minute period have the children name as many different types of strength as they can think of. Write these where the group can see them.

COMIC STRIPS

Give each child a sheet of paper divided as a comic strip.

Ask them to create a comic strip character who displays the characteristic of meekness and draw a strip about him. Have them refer to the list containing the different types of strengths.

Some of the children might prefer to work in teams.

LETTERS TO THE EDITOR

Anyone not finding an interesting assignment from those given could always write a letter to the editor about some aspect of meekness.

FLASH

Using the same brainstorm list as a reference, have the children write a news report about a meek person. You might need to suggest some possibilities.

1. A strong man who refused to fight.
2. A young person who has studied self-defense, ignores the taunts of classmates about some physical characteristic.
3. A girl who does not defend herself in an argument because she would have to reveal a confidence.
4. A young person who was teased for not trying drugs, but was brave enough to save a friend's life.

SPORTS

Have this group write a pretend interview with a sports figure who has given Christ control of his life.

EDITORIAL

Have one volunteer write an editorial called "Who's in Control?"

Shining Star Publications, Copyright © 1988, A division of Good Apple, Inc.   SS847

HUNGER AND THIRST

"Blessed are they which do hunger and thirst after righteousness: for they shall be filled."
Matthew 5:6

Enable your children to experience the joy of feeding others physically, as you help them learn about hungering and thirsting after righteousness.

Children's homes, inner-city missions, people in military service and college students will often welcome homemade cookies. You will need to contact someone in charge of the first two and see what would be helpful, also if there are any restrictions on what can be sent.

If you are sending to people in military service or college students, encourage the children to write notes to be included.

As your group works, talk about:

1. How rarely we really are hungry.
2. Have they ever been hungry for something special, such as homemade cookies?
3. How we need to develop a "taste" for the things of God rather than for a lot of the offensive information and materials we are offered today.

GRANDMOTHER PENFIELD'S SUGAR COOKIES

½ cup butter
1 cup sugar
1 teaspoon vanilla
2 eggs
2½ cups sifted flour
½ teaspoon salt
1 teaspoon baking powder

Cream butter. Add sugar, vanilla and unbeaten eggs. Beat until light. Sift dry ingredients and add to butter mixture. Mix and chill for two hours. Roll thin. Cut and sprinkle with sugar. Bake at 400° until lightly brown around edges.

BLESSED ARE THE MERCIFUL

"Blessed are the merciful: for they shall obtain mercy." Matthew 5:7

CHARACTERS: Dawn   Shannon
              Chrissy   Mom
              Teacher   Class members

SCENE I: (*Dawn looking in locker, and hidden from Shannon and Chrissy who are walking by.*)

SHANNON: Dawn's not my best friend, not really. I only pretend she is because her parents have invited me to go on a camping trip with them this summer.

DAWN: (*Waits for girls to pass, then stares after them.*)

SCENE II: (*Mom in kitchen. Dawn in the next room—perhaps off stage.*)

MOM: Dawn, Shannon is on the phone.

DAWN: Tell her I'll call her back. I'm busy. I'm doing my homework.

MOM: On Saturday, I must be dreaming!

DAWN: Please, Mom!

SCENE III: (*Sunday school. Dawn and Shannon sitting next to each other, but Dawn acting very cool toward her.*)

TEACHER: We are going to talk about relationships this morning. Shannon will you look up Luke 6:27; Chrissy, Romans 12:21; Dawn, Matthew 5:7. Read them and tell us what you think they mean. Anyone else, feel free to share what you think these verses mean. Shannon?

SHANNON: "But I say unto you which hear, Love your enemies, do good to them which hate you." I guess it means we are to love everyone.

CLASS MEMBERS: Yeah, even people who do bad things to us.

TEACHER: Fine. Chrissy, how about your Scripture?

CHRISSY: "Be not overcome of evil, but overcome evil with good." Well, there's lots of evil in the world, but I guess we are not to let it get the best of us. Are we supposed to fight what is wrong by being good?

TEACHER: I think you have the right idea. Dawn, what does your Scripture say?

DAWN: (*Reading slowly.*) "Blessed are the merciful: for they shall obtain mercy." (*Pause.*) I guess we shouldn't try to get even, or hurt people who have hurt us. Maybe we should try to understand why they acted like they did and love them anyway.

TEACHER: (*Smiling.*) That's the way Jesus treats us, isn't it?

CLASS: (*Nods.*)

DAWN: (*Leaning over to Shannon—in stage whisper.*) Want to come over after lunch so we can talk about our camping trip?

PURELY CRAFTY

"Blessed are the pure in heart: for they shall see God." Matthew 5:8

Latch hook is an easy craft for children to do. If you buy canvas on the bolt, "beg and borrow" leftover yarn and extra hooks, it will be an inexpensive group craft project. Mark each canvas with an indelible pen, using the graph below as a guide (This could also be done on plastic canvas.). Tell the children to work the design in dark yarn and the background in a lighter, complementary yarn.

As the children work, discuss the meaning of being pure in heart. Tell the children that it not only means doing the right thing, but doing the right thing for the right reason, such as:

We do not steal—not because we are afraid of being caught,
          but because we know God does not want us to.

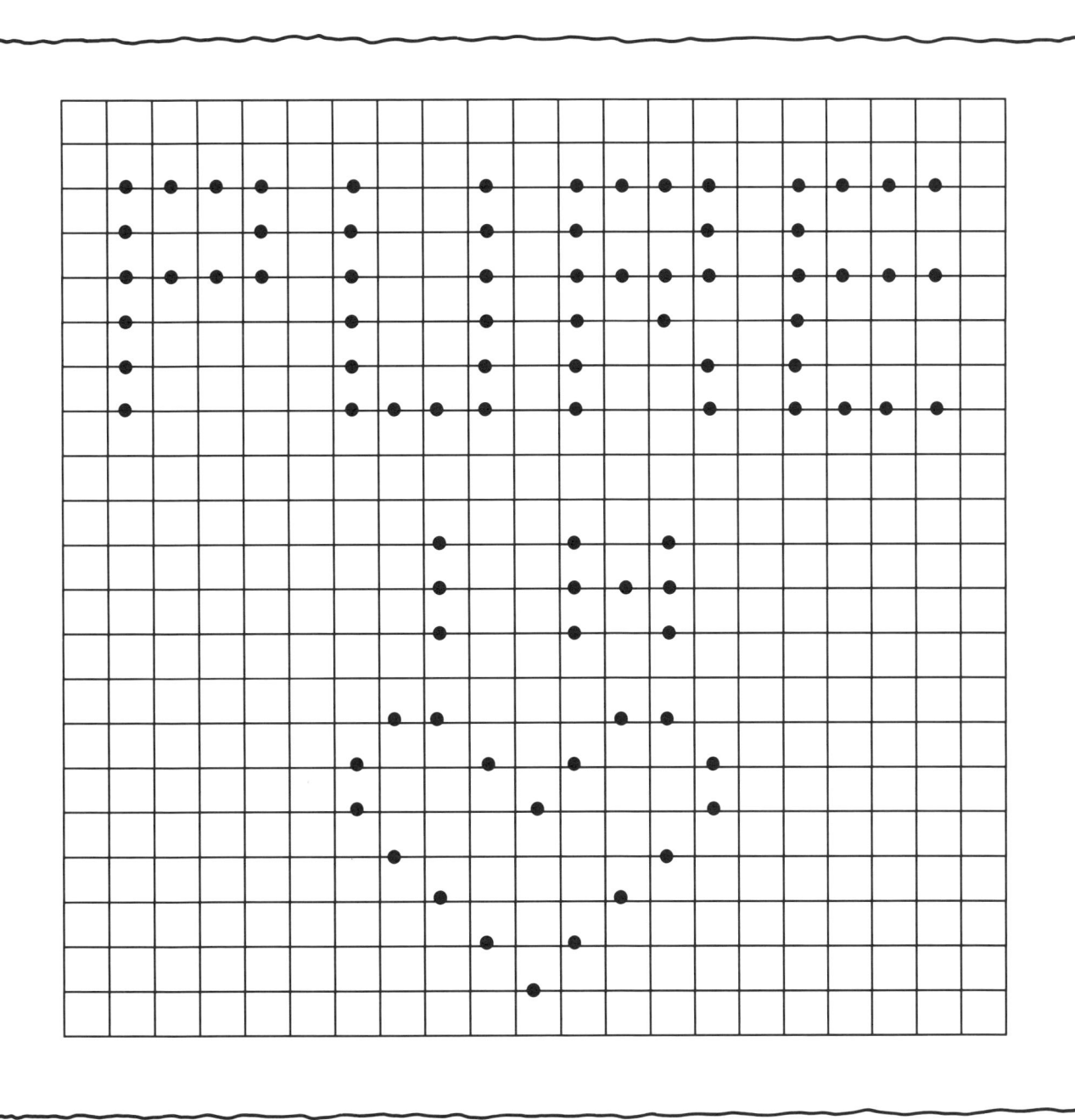

PEACE PROJECTS

"Blessed are the peacemakers: for they shall be called the children of God." Matthew 5:9

Ask the children to discuss what they think peace is. Help them to see that peace is often a very personal problem as well as a worldwide problem.

Present the following projects for them to choose from. Each child may want to do one; or one from each category.

PEACE AT HOME

Peace meal: Plan a family dinner which includes a favorite food of each family member no matter how strange the menu becomes. The rule for the evening is no unpleasant talk at the table. This includes no complaining, criticizing or fighting.

Extra love: Often a lack of peace within a family comes from the unhappiness of one or more family members. Place in a container the name of each family member who is old enough to participate. Let everyone draw a name from the jar. (Make sure no one gets his own.) Tell the family that for one week they are responsible for doing extra nice things in secret for the person whose name they drew.

WITH FRIENDS

Free smiles: Smiles cost nothing, but often we hold on to them like they do. Give smiles away to everyone you meet this week. You may find that you have more friends than you thought.

Secret agent: How many times have you had a friend say something mean or unkind about another friend? Do you feel like you have to tell the other friend what was said? This week don't. Guard it like it was a national secret. You will have become a peacekeeper, if not a peacemaker.

Blabber mouth: Some things were meant to be told and we often forget to tell them. If you hear a friend say something nice about someone else, pass it along. Everyone can use a compliment.

PEACE IN THE WORLD

This category may seem a little beyond the grasp of most of us, but lack of world peace may stem from lack of understanding, and we can do something about that.

Bookworm: Choose a country you know nothing about and learn all you can. Make a poster you can share with the class.

Good Neighbor: There are many people in our country from other lands. If there is someone in your neighborhood or school from another country, spend time getting to know them. Could your family invite a foreign family over for a cookout?

Pen Pal: (for your older students) There are many sources for pen pals from around the world. Check your public library. Why not pick one and use your own personal pen to do something about bettering world understanding? Remember when you write to someone in another country that you are representing the United States and, if you are a Christian, the Lord Jesus Christ.

Pray: Do you pray for peace in the world? If not, why not start today and include it in your daily prayer time? Look in the newspapers and watch the news so you can be specific about things and people for whom you pray.

PERSECUTED

"Blessed are they which are persecuted for righteousness' sake: for theirs is the kingdom of heaven."
Matthew 5:10

Fill in the bubbles to demonstrate how a person being persecuted might respond in a positive way.

Ha, ha! He's going to church!

Let me copy your homework, or I won't be your friend!

I'm going to take this candy bar and you'd better not tell!

HAPPY HIKERS

Make an opportunity for your group to spread around some of the happiness about which they have been learning. Nursing homes or senior citizens groups are often eager to have children present short programs.

Ask them to wear hiking clothes as costumes. Make large name tags for each child to wear. If you will be presenting your program in more than one place, cover these with clear Con-Tact paper.

The program could consist of:

> ♪ **THEME SONG** ♪
> (sung to the tune "I'm a Tramping")
> We are hiking, hiking,
>   To share Jesus' joy with you.
> We are hiking, hiking
>   So you can know His happiness too.

Reciting the beautitudes using the Jesus puppet on page 91.

Singing "Beatitudes" on page 90.

Presenting *Blessed Are the Merciful* play on page 96.

Saying good-bye.

Saying good-bye is important, because many people in the audience will want to spend a little time with the children. Teach your group to shake hands and smile. Be on guard so you can politely rescue any of the children from someone who wants to keep them too long or becomes overly emotional. A friendly, "I'm glad you've enjoyed Tony's visit, but we must be going," will generally do the trick.

THE BIBLE TEACHES US HOW TO PRAY

Bulletin Board Idea

WHERE? WHY? WHAT? WHEN? HOW?

PURPOSE: To establish questions in the minds of the children that these activities will answer.

PROCEDURE:
1. Make background of light colored paper or fabric.
2. Using an overhead projector, enlarge the pattern of praying child. Mount it on an oval of colored construction paper which will contrast with the background.
3. Cut letters and question marks from construction paper.

EXTENDED ACTIVITY: As the children complete the activities in this chapter, have them illustrate or write sentences that answer the questions and attach to the bulletin board.

WHERE SHOULD WE PRAY?

"... enter into thy closet ...." Matthew 6:6

SCRIPTURE SEARCH

Have the children look up the following Scriptures to find out where Jesus prayed:

Matthew 6:6
Matthew 14:23
Matthew 26:36-45
Mark 1:35

REQUIREMENTS

Let the class discuss what makes a good place to pray. List the ideas on the board. Be sure the children understand you are talking about a set place for a personal prayer time, but they may pray anywhere.

MY IDEAL

On index cards have children write descriptions of places they consider perfect for praying and reading the Bible.

MY REALITY

Provide everyone with a sheet of drawing paper. Have them draw an outline of the inside of their house. Ask them to mark each place in their house where they pray with a "P." Encourage them to locate other good places and mark them with a "G."

Discuss what could be done to turn new places for quiet times into good places for prayer.

Remind the children that at certain times of the year a porch or a spot in the yard also makes a good place to pray.

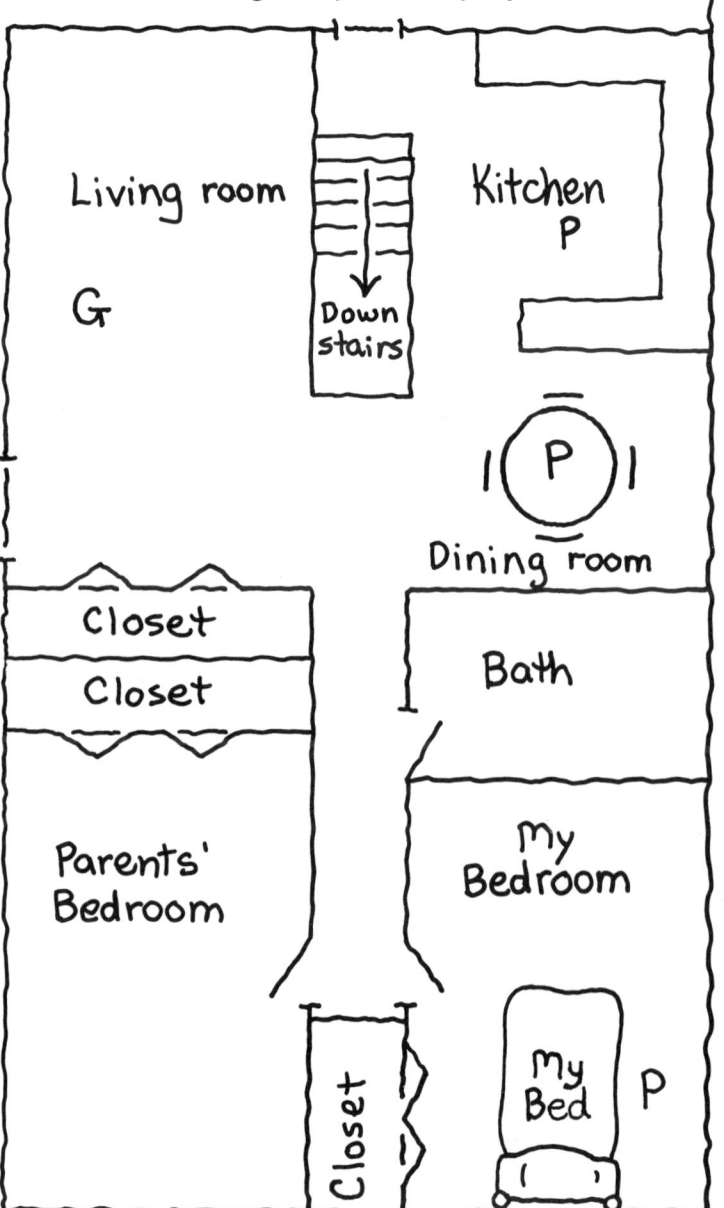

PROPER PRAYER ATTITUDES

"... I will pray with the spirit, and I will pray with the understanding also...."
I Corinthians 14:15

DICTIONARY CHECK:
Bring several different dictionaries to class. Let the children look up and compare definitions of the word "attitude." Ask them to compose their own definition. Brainstorm and create a list of different attitudes.

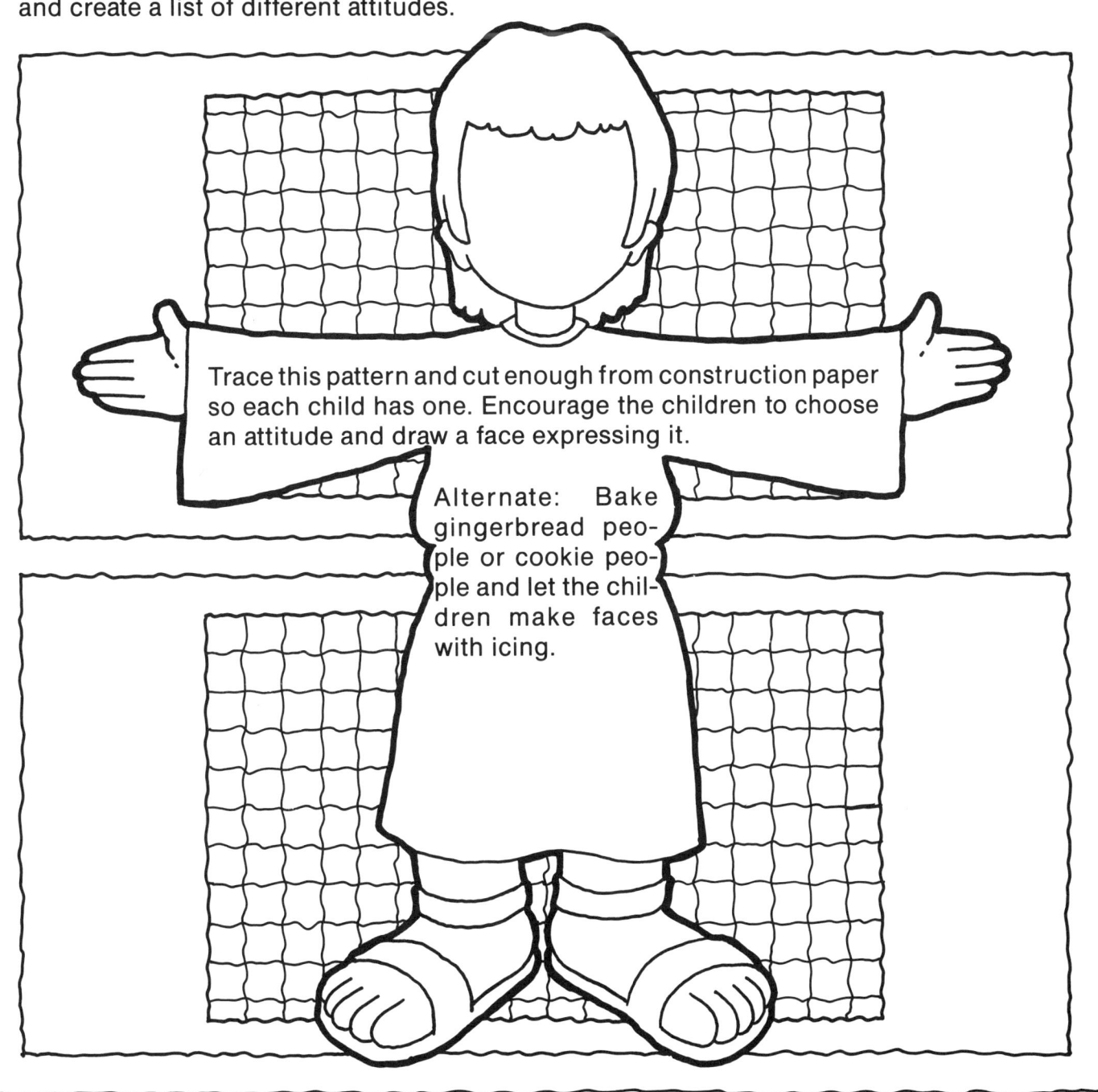

Trace this pattern and cut enough from construction paper so each child has one. Encourage the children to choose an attitude and draw a face expressing it.

Alternate: Bake gingerbread people or cookie people and let the children make faces with icing.

Line these men up against a background or on a table. Have the children choose the "dolls" or cookies which seem to be in the best attitude for prayer.

Shining Star Publications, Copyright © 1988, A division of Good Apple, Inc.

SS847

THE LORD'S PRAYER

Text from Matthew 6:9-13
Music by
Helen Friesen

PRAYER AND PRAISE

"... Hallowed be thy name."   Matthew 6:9

TALK ABOUT IT

Lead the group in a discussion of what praise is and is not. Ask them to think about how much of their personal prayer time is spent in praise.

HYMNAL SEARCH

Provide church hymnals for each child. Ask them to go through and list hymns which are really prayers of praise.

PRAISE YOUR NEIGHBOR

Have the children sit in a circle. Give them a few minutes to think and then give the person sitting on their right a compliment.

Point out that we all enjoy being praised. We are smart or pretty or strong because of the way God has made us. Such traits as kindness or patience should be acknowledged too. They are often the result of the training we have been given at home and school.

Remind the children that God truly does deserve our praise.

PRAISE SONG

Using simple, familiar tunes such as nursery rhyme songs, ask the children to try their hand at writing a praise song.

PRAISE POEMS

Challenge the children to write praise poems or acrostics. Use the following for the acrostics or let the children come up with their own.

F	God	W
Alpha	R	Omega
T	E	R
H	A	T
E	T	H
R		Y

PRAISE WORDS

Spread fingerpaint on appropriate paper or shaving cream on top of a table. Let the children enjoy working with it for a few minutes. Then, challenge them to write in the fingerpaint as many praise words as they can think of in three minutes. Have them share their words. You may want to make a list on the board.

THE THINGS OF THE KINGDOM

"Thy kingdom come...." Matthew 6:10

LEARNING ABOUT...

To help the children learn as much as possible about the "things of the kingdom" in your congregation's ministry, take a tour of the church building. Be sure to include displays of mission photographs, areas where food or other supplies for benevolent use are stored, ministers' offices, secretaries' offices and the church kitchen. Be prepared to answer questions about what goes on in each area or ask a staff member to be available for questions. For example: Is the church kitchen used for social purposes only or are ministry functions such as "Meals on Wheels" or funeral dinners conducted from there?

If your church is also involved in nearby ministries such as inner-city missions, a food kitchen or child care, you may want to extend your tour to include them. Slides or pictures can provide information about projects which cannot be visited.

Different children will probably become interested in different areas. Divide them into groups according to interest or let them tour as individuals.

ILLUSTRATING WHAT WAS LEARNED

Provide each group or individual with poster board, paints, markers, construction paper, glue, etc. Encourage them to make a poster featuring the area of the work of God's kingdom about which they are most interested.

Display these where the congregation will have an opportunity to see them. Perhaps the interest of the children will spread and help recruit workers for some of these ministries.

Be prepared for the interest of the children to spread beyond the poster drawing stage. If they indicate desire to do something to help in one of these areas, contact someone in charge and ask for something the children can do.

CLASS QUILT

Give each child a pre-washed 12" square of permanent press muslin. Let them decide whether to trace their own hand to form a praying hand or one of the designs below. (You may trace these and cut patterns from cardboard.) Using a permanent marker, liquid embroidery tube or embroidery thread and needle (this will take longer), have them color their block and add their names. A teacher can take these home to stitch together, forming a quilt. Blank blocks may be added to make an even number, if needed. Quilt batting and a backing may be added. At the next meeting of your group the quilt can be tacked using embroidery thread. This will make a nice wall hanging or gift for the nursery.

DAILY BREAD

"Give us this day our daily bread." Matthew 6:11

BAKING BREAD

Let children make bread from a recipe or frozen dough. Yeast is probably the most fun to work with, but takes a long time from start to finish. You might want to make the dough yourself and leave the kneading to the children. The corn bread recipe from page 86 could also be used.

TASTING PARTY

Ask the children to bring an unusual type of bread to class for a tasting party. As you eat, discuss the origin of the different breads. You may want to bring along several cookbooks. Let the children look up various bread recipes and compare ingredients.

Discuss a diet of bread only and observe the children's reactions. Remind them that bread is often used to refer to food as a whole.

VISIT A BAKERY

Is there a bakery in your area that will let the children pay a visit? This would make a nice outing.

TODAY'S DAILY BREAD

Nutritionists recommend that we eat foods from the four basic food groups each day. List these where the children can see them:

Bread and cereal
Fruits and vegetables
Milk and dairy products
Meat and other protein foods

Ask the children to list the foods they have eaten from each food group during the past twenty-four hours. Suggest they share a time of silent prayer thanking God for providing their daily "bread."

Have children cut out magazine pictures of food from the four main food groups for a collage. (Labels from canned foods could also be used.)

PRACTICAL PRAYER PRACTICES

Encourage the children to make and use some of the following prayer reminders and aids to help develop good prayer habits.

PRAYER AID BIBLEMARK

PRAYER DIARY

Pass out small notebooks and encourage the children to use them as prayer diaries. Show them how to record what they prayed for during the day.

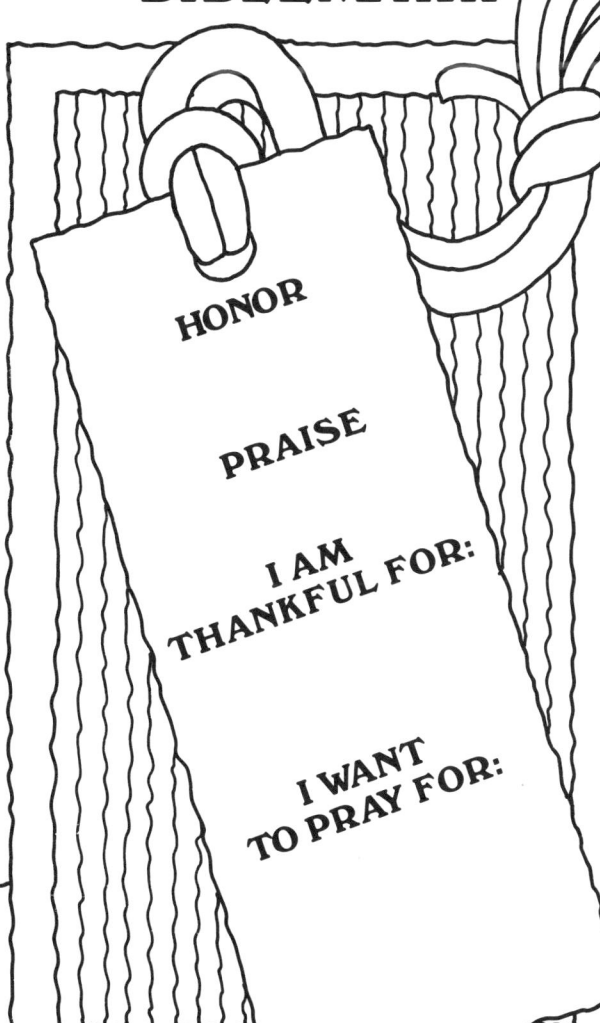

LITTLE THINGS

Pass out index cards (colored are nice). Show the children how to fold these so they will stand up. Let them decorate the cards with colored pens and/or stickers.

INDEX CARDS

Give each child four index cards. Have him label them: Praise, Thanksgiving, Problems, People. Encourage children to list their prayer concerns and keep these for use in their personal prayer time. Discuss ways in which prayer is answered. Suggest to children they might write down times they feel their prayers have been answered.

Stickers of praying hands (either purchased or cut from Con-Tact paper) can be used on mirrors, bedside lamps and car dashboards.

THE POWER OF FORGIVENESS

"And forgive us our debts, as we forgive our debtors."   Matthew 6:12

Matthew 6:12 coupled with verses 14 and 15 are some of the most important teachings of our Lord. These verses contain a principle that is best learned while young—forgiveness. Many adults struggle for years to believe in God's forgiveness. Perhaps this is because they have not understood and practiced the basic requirement for forgiveness. To receive God's forgiveness for our sins, we must forgive those who have mistreated us.

ROLE-PLAY

It sometimes seems as if our world is a world of getting even. Many live as if they believe the Golden Rule read, "Do unto others something worse than they did to you." Let the children play out some of the following situations. Discuss the principle of forgiveness before they begin.

I
Participants: Brian, Jacob and teacher
Problem: Jacob repeatedly steals items from Brian's school box.

II
Participants: Dawn and Marcy
Problem: Dawn makes fun of Marcy because she is _____ (a physical characteristic that does not apply to someone in your class).

III
Participants: Terry, Sam and teacher
Problem: Everytime the teacher turns his back, Terry punches, trips or makes a face at Sam.

IV
Participants: Child and Mom
Problem: This child has never met his dad because his dad deserted the family before he was born. The child blames his dad for the financial problems of the family. (If this situation is too close to real life for one or more children in your class, discard it.)

When the role-playing is finished, remind the children that some of these problems cannot be solved easily or maybe at all, but that most situations will improve if we forgive the person who has mistreated us. Praying for that person is often the first step toward forgiveness.

PRAYER-A-GRAM

"Pray without ceasing."   I Thessalonians 5:17

Reproduce "prayer-a-grams" below for each child.

Demonstrate how to fill them out and encourage the children to send them to people for whom they have prayed.

To:_____

Just thought you would like to know that someone thought about you and prayed for you today. That someone was:

_____

". . . men ought always to pray . . . ."   Luke 18:1

To:_____

Just thought you would like to know that someone thought about you and prayed for you today. That someone was:

_____

". . . men ought always to pray . . . ."   Luke 18:1

PRAYER WALK

Find a secluded area of your prayer walk where your "props" will not be disturbed. If there is no place on church property, think about church members' homes.

Schedule the walk at your regular meeting or, perhaps, early morning. If you choose to do the latter, a simple picnic breakfast could be served afterwards.

The day (or a few hours) before the walk, scout and plan the route. Take along index cards, plastic sandwich bags and masking tape. Carefully look for things which can be used to bring forth prayers of thanksgiving and praise. Bird's nests, a clump of flowers or an especially majestic tree could be used. Try to schedule these toward the beginning of your walk. Write appropriate prayer sentences, place them in a plastic bag (in case of rain) and tape securely, placing in a visible spot.

In a dark secluded spot, leave a reminder to pray for those in sorrow or who are sick.

Shortly before the walk begins, re-check the route to be sure everything is still in place. If you are going to have an adult guide small groups, discuss the route and decide if the guides are simply to show the way and read the prayer reminders, or to actually lead the prayers. Be sure to space the children so no one feels rushed.

If you have older children who can read the prayer reminders themselves, simply point out the route and let them follow it.

At the end, provide well-spaced rocks, cushions or plastic bags for seats if the ground is damp.

As people finish, they can continue in personal prayer and thought while sitting down.

You may want to begin singing together quietly as children return.

Don't forget to retrieve all the clues and items left on the prayer trail after the prayer walk is completed.

A place that gives a wide view, such as, a lawn or the sky, is a good area for placing a reminder to pray for certain missionaries around the world. If possible, name missionaries the children know, or know about.

THE BIBLE TEACHES ABOUT PEOPLE LIKE US

Bulletin Board Idea

PEOPLE LIKE US

PURPOSE: To help the children realize that meeting or learning about Jesus has always made a difference in people's lives.

PROCEDURE:
1. Make background of bright red crepe paper. Cut letters from black construction paper.
2. Search used Sunday school visuals for pictures which could represent Peter and Andrew and other fishermen disciples, Matthew the tax collector, and Luke, the physician. Mount pictures on construction paper ovals.
3. From magazines, cut pictures of modern factory workers, executives, doctors and nurses, etc. Mount pictures on construction paper ovals.
4. Mount pictures of your children on small ovals of construction paper and place on bulletin board.
5. Cut construction paper "Bibles" to scatter around.

WHO AM I?

Jesus worked with and taught people from many different occupations and backgrounds. His disciples did the same.

Show the children how to write "Who Am I" questions. For example: Someone might write the following about Simon Peter:
1. My brother brought me to Jesus. Who am I?
2. My brother and I were fishermen. Who am I?
3. Jesus once told me to walk on water. Who am I?
4. I once said I did not know who Jesus was. Who am I?
5. I preached the first sermon after Jesus returned to heaven. Who am I?

REFERENCES

SHEPHERDS: Luke 2:8; Luke 2:20

SIMEON: Luke 2:25-32

ANNA: Luke 2:36-38

JOHN THE BAPTIST: Matthew 3:1; Matthew 3:14-16; John 3:26-30

SYROPHOENICIAN WOMAN: Mark 7:25-30; Matthew 15:22-28

ZACCHAEUS: Luke 19:2-10

LEVI OR MATTHEW: Mark 2:14-22; Luke 6:15

CENTURION: Matthew 8:5-13

LYDIA: Acts 16:14, 15

NICODEMUS: John 3:1-13

RICH YOUNG MAN: Matthew 19:16-22; Mark 10:17-22

Let the children work as individuals, in twos, or in small groups to do the following activities:
1. Give them the name of the person and the Scripture references and ask them to write at least three "Who Am I" questions about that person.
2. Give them the Scripture references only and have them discover who the person is before learning more about him and writing the "Who Am I" questions. (The first verse given should contain the name of only one person.)

After the children have written their questions, let them take turns quizzing classmates.

Shining Star Publications, Copyright © 1988, A division of Good Apple, Inc.   SS847

BIBLE DOLL

"... be ye doers of the word, and not hearers only ...." James 1:22

SEAM LINE

LEAVE ONE SIDE OPEN TO STUFF

CUT 2 PIECES ON FOLD

LEG

CUT 2 PIECES ON FOLD

ARM

CUT 2 PIECES ON FOLD

Using information from "Who Am I", let each child choose a person, or type of person, Jesus might have met and make a doll.

Cutting the body parts from muslin or broadcloth, either stitch, or let the children stitch, the pieces together. Clip along curves and turn. The pieces can then be stuffed with poly-fil and the arms and legs joined to the body.

Provide markers, fabric, felt, ribbon and other materials that the children can use to dress their dolls. Faces can be drawn on or left blank.

LET'S WRITE

"If any man serve me, let him follow me . . . ." — John 12:26

Pretending to be a person living in Jesus' time, let the children choose to do one or more of the following creative writing activities.

DIARY ENTRY

Record the first time the person met Jesus, or the change Jesus made in his/her life. (For someone who lived during the period of the early church, it could be reworded "the first time that person heard about Jesus".)

POSTCARD

Pass out index cards. Tell the children to write a postcard describing a meeting with Jesus. Illustrate the backside of the "post card."

LETTER

The above idea can be extended by using a letter format. Give the children a letter form to follow.

SUMMER VACATION

Ask the children to pretend that they are a boy or girl of their own age living in the time of Jesus. Have them write a composition, "What I Did on My Summer Vacation," incorporating the idea that they met or heard Jesus teach during the time they were out of school.

These could be read in front of the class or posted on a bulletin board.

TELEGRAM

A third way to use the same idea is to have them write a telegram. It should convey the excitement and influence of the meeting.

Reproduce forms to be used (on yellow paper, if possible).

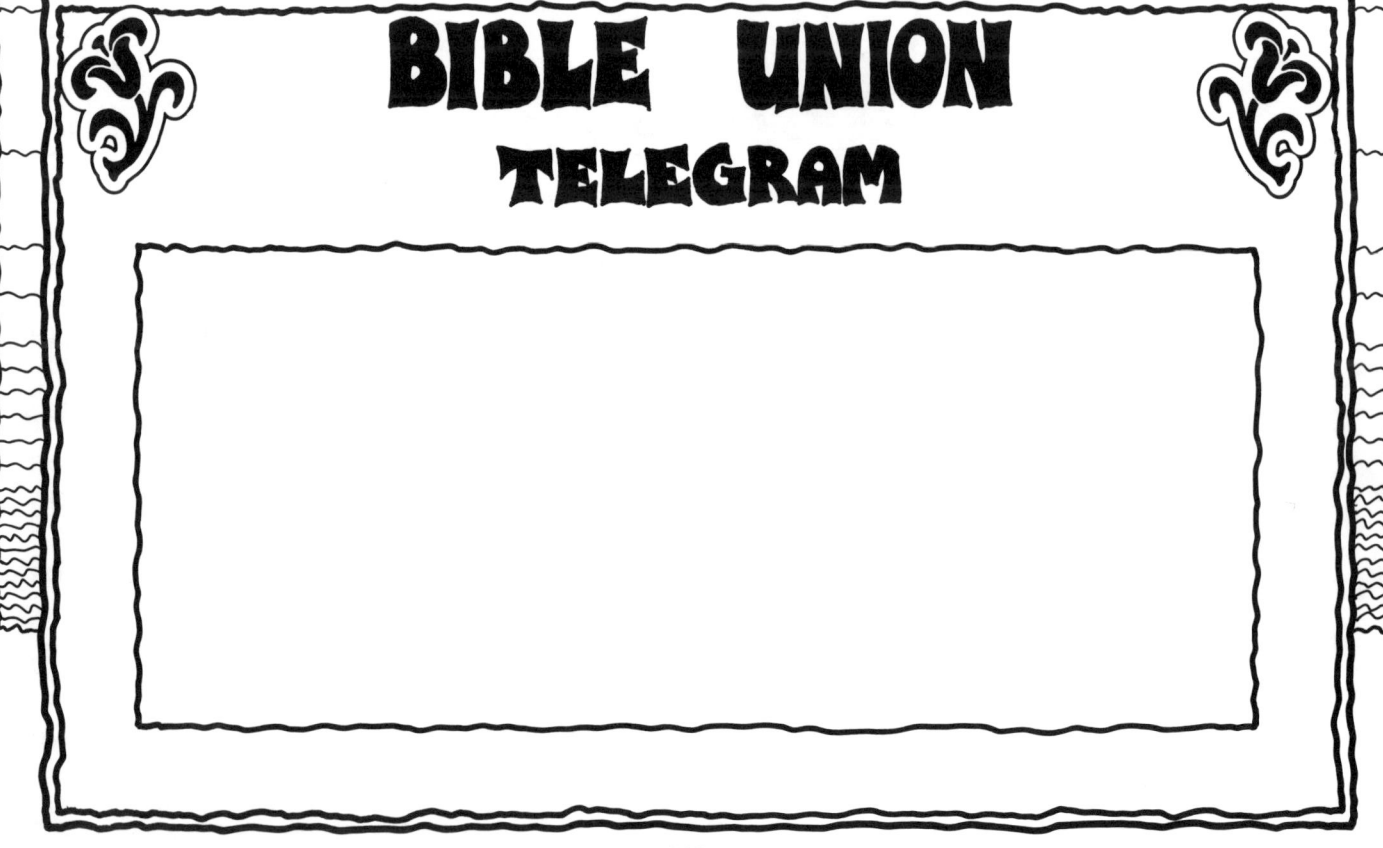

BIBLE UNION TELEGRAM

PUZZLE PAGE

"... be followers together of me ...." Philippians 3:17

Search the following letters to find how people earned their living in Bible times. Can you find these occupations: farmer, fisherman, tax collector, physician, merchant, innkeeper, shepherd

X	F	A	R	M	E	R	T	V	M	A	C
Z	I	I	N	N	K	E	E	P	E	R	M
I	S	W	E	R	T	Y	U	I	R	V	B
P	H	Y	S	I	C	I	A	N	C	O	P
U	E	S	D	F	G	H	J	K	H	K	L
W	R	Z	X	C	V	B	N	M	A	B	C
U	M	T	R	E	W	Q	P	U	N	L	S
T	A	X	C	O	L	L	E	C	T	O	R
V	N	M	N	S	H	E	P	H	E	R	D
L	E	V	M	S	O	E	C	K	H	Y	T

HOW MANY WORDS?

How many smaller words can you find in the following Bible times occupation?

FISHERMAN

___ ___ ___ ___ ___
___ ___ ___ ___ ___
___ ___ ___ ___ ___
___ ___ ___ ___ ___

By rearranging the letters, how many words can you make? Do not use any letter more than once.

___ ___ ___ ___ ___
___ ___ ___ ___ ___
___ ___ ___ ___ ___
___ ___ ___ ___ ___

DISCUSS

1. What occupations help prepare people to serve Jesus? Why?
2. Can you think of other Bible times occupations?
3. What are some occupations people of today have that didn't exist during Bible times?

Shining Star Publications, Copyright © 1988, A division of Good Apple, Inc.   SS847

RADIO PROGRAM

"... they remembered his words," — Luke 24:8

Tape a radio talk show and play it for the children. Ask them to list all of the people participating. This may include an announcer, a host, several persons to be interviewed and someone to do commercials.

Let the children plan a program of their own. Interview "guests" from Jesus' time or early days of the church. These could include those who were taught by Jesus or were influenced by His early followers. The children may want to include some appropriate music.

Help the "interviewer" include questions about background, occupation or everyday life and how Jesus' teaching and influence changed their thoughts and activities. Sample questions might be:

1. Can you tell us about the work you do each day?
2. When did you first hear Jesus teach (or hear about Jesus)?
3. What did you think about Jesus?
4. Can you think of anything about your everyday life that has changed since you learned about Jesus?
5. Do you feel differently about other people since you learned about Jesus?

Have the children chosen to be interviewed, think through their character. Ask them to try to imagine an ordinary day in the life of a fisherman such as Peter or a woman such as Lydia. What might they have thought about as they worked before they met Jesus? How might this have changed later? If possible, have some simple books about life in Bible times available to help them form mental images. Check the children's section of the library. Ask your children's librarian for help.

Practice the program including music and commercials. Make any changes the children feel are needed.

Before taping the program, remind the children to be quiet when others are talking. Print an "On the Air" sign to help them remember. Turn sign over when the tape recorder is turned off.

After the tape is made, let the children take turns sharing it at home with their families.

ALTERNATIVE

If there is a video recorder available, the children might enjoy doing a "television" program. This will involve more elaborate planning, as costumes will be needed. (Check with the director of the last church Christmas program.)

THE BIBLE AND ART

"... his word was with power." Luke 4:32

We have no biblical record of any contact between Jesus and the artists of that time. There is no doubt, however, that all the teachings of the Bible have greatly influenced many artists since then.

ART SHOW

Check your local library for books of art which may center on religious themes. Many libraries also have paintings and prints which may be borrowed. Ask church members for pictures and, perhaps, statues. (Do not borrow anything of value.) Acquire prints of some of the more familiar pictures such as "Jesus and the Children" or "Jesus Knocking at the Door". Arrange an exhibit of the paintings, statues and books. Let the children spend time looking at the exhibit.

After examining the display, call the group together to discuss what they have seen. Let each child tell what his favorite was, and why. Be prepared to find the biblical reference which inspired the word.

MUSEUM VISIT

If you have a local art museum, check to see if they have an exhibit of religious art. If so, arrange a visit. Allow time for discussion after the visit.

THE CHILDREN AS ARTISTS

Provide paints, paper or canvases, drawing pencils and clay. Let the children choose a medium to express their ideas about how:

1. Jesus touched the lives of people who met Him.

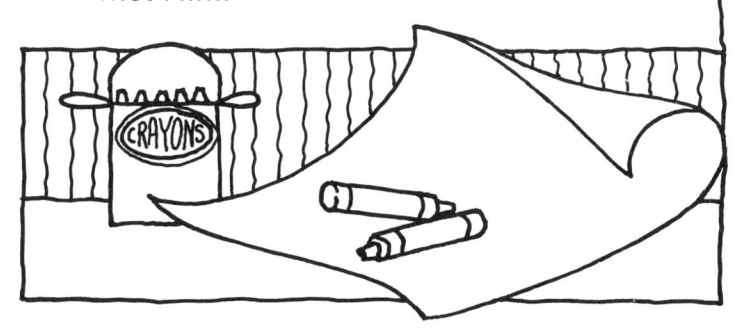

2. How Jesus' teachings in the Bible are still changing lives today.

3. Something in their lives which was learned from the Bible.

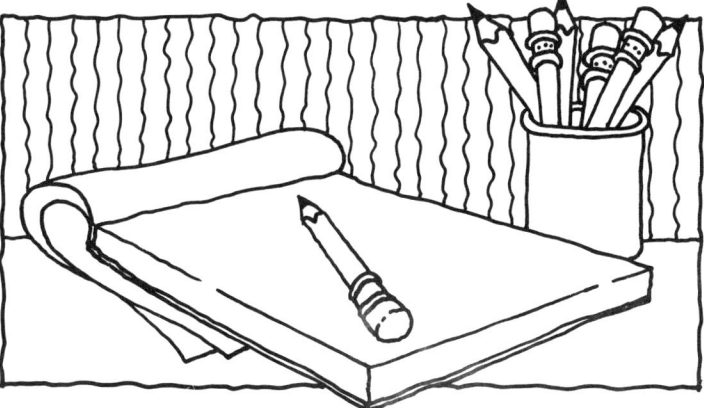

Shining Star Publications, Copyright © 1988, A division of Good Apple, Inc. SS847

GAMES, FINGERPLAYS AND ACTION RHYMES

"Let the word of Christ dwell in you richly in all wisdom. . . ." Colossians 3:16

THIS IS THE WAY

Sung to the tune of: "This Is the Way We Wash Our Clothes"

This is the way they fished for food,
fished for food,
fished for food.
This is the way they fished for food,
back in Bible times.
(*Cast nets and pull them in.*)

This is the way they baked their bread,
baked their bread,
baked their bread.
This is the way they baked their bread,
back in Bible times.
(*Knead "bread."*)

Other verses could include:
Wove their cloth
(*Push shuttle back and forth.*)

Watched their sheep (*Use staffs.*)

Learned about (or from) Jesus
(*Sit quietly.*)

CHANGES

When Jesus talked to people,
(*Hold up fingers on left hand.*)

Their lives were often changed.
(*Hold up fingers on right hand.*)

They grew more kind and loving, (*Touch fingers together as if greeting each other.*)

And their plans were rearranged.
(*Use both hands to appear to be praying.*)

When people read the Bible,
(*Hold hands together and open as a Bible.*)

Their lives are often changed.
(*Point to self.*)

They grow more kind and loving,
(*Touch fingers together as if greeting.*)

And their plans are rearranged.
(*Use both hands as if praying.*)

JESUS CHOSE

Give each child a Bible occupation. Explain that when they are chosen they must stand and choose someone to fill that role.

Sing to the tune of: "Mary Had a Little Lamb."

Jesus taught a fisherman, fisherman, fisherman.

Jesus taught a fisherman, to live the way God planned.

Other people to be named might be:

Shepherd   Innkeeper
Weaver of cloth   Tax collector
Man of law   Shipbuilder
Temple priest   Tentmaker
Homemaker   Seller of purple

The last verse could be:

The Bible teaches me today, me today, me today.
The Bible teaches me today, to walk in Jesus' way.

THE EARLY CHURCH

"... the disciples were called Christians first in Antioch."   Acts 11:26

BIBLICAL TIMES

Help the children learn about what a gathering of Christians might have been like when the church was new. Provide books about life in Bible times, Bible dictionaries and Bible encyclopedias. We are all so accustomed to church buildings, Bibles, bulletins and other aids to worship that it is hard to imagine that it has not always been so. Of course, many early church gatherings took place in the temple court or in homes.

Let the children make a house (minus roof) from a sturdy carton. If there is printing on it, it can be painted. Using chenille wire and scraps of cloth, have them make the congregation.

AN EARLY WORSHIP SERVICE

Discuss how an early worship might have been conducted. Acts 2:42 is the closest thing we have to an order of worship. Let the children talk about how each element mentioned in that verse might have been handled. You may need to remind them that the New Testament was not completed for a long time, but different books were actually letters to certain churches. Ask, "How do you think a congregation felt when someone delivered a letter from Paul to them?"

MAKE A SCROLL

Printing is also something we take for granted. Make a scroll from two paper towel tubes (dowels make more elegant scrolls) and a long strip of paper. Let the children take turns copying one of the shorter letters such as Philemon or II John. Remind them that the writing tools early Christians worked with were harder to use. Let them speculate on how long it would have taken to make a copy of I Corinthians or Hebrews. Count how many different Bibles are in your classroom at this time. If your sanctuary has pew Bibles and is unoccupied at this time, count them. Give thanks for the blessing of having Bibles so available today.

OTHERS

Remind the children that not all Christians today have Bibles readily available. Perhaps you would like to start a class project to help an organization provide Bibles to people in other lands.

Shining Star Publications, Copyright © 1988, A division of Good Apple, Inc.   SS847

OUR CHURCH

"... If a man love me, he will keep my words...." John 14:23

THE STAFF

Ask members of the church staff to visit and briefly tell the children what they do.

OUR CHURCH QUESTIONNAIRE

Name: _____

Occupation: _____

Do you think studying the Bible and knowing Jesus makes a difference in the way you go about your everyday occupation?

Yes No

Position (or positions) in the church:

Other comments:

_____
_____
_____

THE PEOPLE

Plan to do spot interviews of the congregation as they leave worship some Sunday morning. The congregation should be made aware of this through the church newsletter, bulletin and/or from the pulpit. They should be told, "Some of our young people are trying to learn more about our congregation. They will be asking some of you to fill out a brief questionnaire as you leave. Don't feel you have to participate if you do not have time or do not want to participate."

Arm your children with questionnaires, pencils and a box to collect completed questionnaires and pencils. At each exit, station at least one child to hand out questionnaires and one to hold the box and retrieve the pencils. Remind them to smile and say "Thank you."

AT A LATER DATE

Let the children make a list of all the different occupations, jobs done in the church and the number of people who answered "yes" to the question. You might want to make these statistics available to the church paper.

Save the questionnaires to be used with a Testimony Tea. (See page 124.)

REMINDER BOARD

"... receive with meekness the engrafted word. ..." — James 1:21

Give each child an 8" x 12" piece of colorful poster board. Let them decorate the edges with markers using the theme "The Bible Guides Me Every Day."

Help them to cover their boards with clear Con-Tact paper. Punch two holes in the top and put string through them. Show the children how water-based markers can be used to write on their reminder board and then be washed off.

THE BIBLE GUIDES ME EVERY DAY NOTES

- HOME
- JOYS
- WHERE I GO

TESTIMONY TEA

"Hold fast the form of sound words. . . ." II Timothy 1:13

Using the questionnaires from page 122, ask four or five people from completely different walks of life to share with your group in a Testimony Tea.

Explain that you would like each person to briefly tell the following about himself:

1. How the person learned about Jesus and when he became a Christian.
2. What the person's occupation is and a little about it. (Remind the people about the ages of the children they will be talking to and ask them to keep all explanations simple.)
3. How the person believes Jesus and studying the Bible has made a difference in the way he does his job.

A sample of the type of testimony you would like for them to give is: "Hello, my name is Bob Smith. I was raised by Christian parents who taught me about Jesus all my life. I became a Christian when I was twelve. Today I am a fireman. I work at the fire station near the church. I think being a Christian and studying the Bible helps me be a better fireman because I know God's promises and I can pray even when I am fighting a big fire. Also, I am careful about little things because I know Jesus expects me to do my best."

Serve simple refreshments such as cookies and punch. (Let the children help with bringing refreshments, decorating and serving.)

Set up chairs in small groups (one group for each speaker). Ask the speakers to visit each group and encourage the children to ask them questions. Before the tea begins, give your guests the following discussion starters in case the children are shy:

1. What do you think you would like to be when you are grown up?
2. Do you think reading the Bible and knowing Jesus will make you a better _____?

Let the children present the speakers with a small token of appreciation at closing time. These could be Christian bookmarks, desk plaques, calendars or other daily helps.

BIBLE FACT GAMES

HOW TO USE GAME CARDS

To get the most value from them, the game cards on pages 131-142 need preparation time.

1. The division indication on the back upper right-hand corner needs to be color coded in the following manner.
   Law-red
   Old Testament history-blue
   Poetry-purple
   Major prophecy-green
   Minor prophecy-brown
   Gospels-yellow
   New Testament history-blue
   Letters-orange
   New Testament prophecy-green

   This can be done by lightly coloring over the division name with crayon or marker.

2. Using clear Con-Tact paper, cover both sides of the cards before cutting. This will make them more durable and easier to use.
3. Cut along lines.
4. Using a sharp paper punch, make a hole where indicated, (0), in each back lower left-hand corner.

GAMES TO BE PLAYED

SORTING GAMES

1. Letting the children look at the backs of the cards, see how quickly they can put the cards into the proper category of Old Testament and New Testament. As they become more proficient in this, challenge them to sort without looking at the back.
2. For a group version of the game, divide the children into two groups. Working in relay fashion, let the children race to put the cards in the proper category. The group completing the task accurately in the shortest amount of time will be declared the winners.
3. Using the color codes, let the children work on learning the smaller categories.
4. The first two activities may be used with the smaller categories as well.

STRINGING GAMES

Provide a thin shoestring for each category.

1. As a learning activity, let the children practice stringing large or small categories using the backs as guides.
2. Label each string with a category, perhaps pinning one end under the label to a bulletin board. Divide the cards (mixed up) between the children. Time them to see how long it takes them to get the cards in the proper order on the proper strings. Be sure to place the strings far apart and be prepared for a good deal of confusion. If the children enjoy this game, you might want to play it at the end of class for a few weeks. Chart the improvement in accuracy and time.

WHAT BOOK AM I?

1. As the children become more and more familiar with the books of the Bible, they will probably be ready for this game. Divide the class into two groups. Place a bell on a table between the groups. Tell the children that as soon as someone recognizes a book from the Bible, they are to run for the bell. If they can properly identify the book their side will get a point. Stress the fact that only one person in each group needs to run for the bell. Slowly read the "clues" as follows:

   a. This book is in the Old Testament.
   b. It is a book of poetry.
   c. It is the nineteenth book in the Bible.
   d. It is the second book in the poetry category. (Continued on page 141.)

Shining Star Publications, Copyright © 1988, A division of Good Apple, Inc. SS847

MUSICAL GAMES

BOOK WALK

Record the "Old Testament Books" song on page 127 and the "New Testament Books" song on page 128.

Using small pieces of rolled masking tape or double stick tape, place the books of either the Old or New Testament in a circle on the floor. Show the children how to walk beside them, cakewalk fashion, while the music plays. Explain that they are to stop when the music stops. If any child was on the last book mentioned before the music stopped he is the winner. Ask him to read the information on the back side of his card (or tell you what he knows about that book) before giving him an award. (A piece of candy or a sticker is sufficient.) The tape can be rewound and stopped at different points until every child has had an opportunity to win at least once.

STAND UP

Give each child one or two cards from the game cards of the song you will be using. Have the children sit on chairs in a circle. Tell them that when the book whose name they are holding is sung, they are to stand and then sit down immediately. Use the musical tape from the above game, and then let the children do the same activity while they are singing the songs.

NEXT?

Either using the tape or playing and singing the songs yourself, stop occasionally and point to a child. Ask that child to tell you the next book.

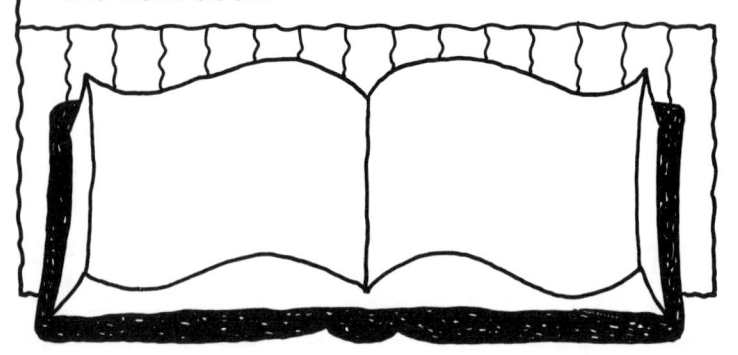

BIBLE PASS

While playing one of the songs, let the children stand in a circle. Give them a Bible (remind them that they should treat it carefully) to pass as the songs are sung. When the music stops, the child holding the Bible is to try to locate the last book mentioned, as quickly as possible.

BEANBAG TOSS

Using one beanbag let the children toss it back and forth as the music is played. Encourage them to sing the words as they play.

BEANBAG PASS

Standing in a circle, let the children pass the beanbag around in time to the music. Again encourage them to sing the words as they play.

LINE UP

Tape a book of the Bible card (use game cards or make your own) to the back of each child. Make sure the books you use are in sequence. Playing the song representing the books you used, tell the children to put themselves in the proper order before the song is ended. Do not tell the children which book is on their back. Extend the game by switching cards or adding different ones.

OLD TESTAMENT BOOKS
by Beulahmae Marchbanks

Gen-e-sis, Ex-o-dus, Lev-it-i-cus, Num-bers, Deut-er-on-om-y, Josh-u-a, Jud-ges, Ruth,

First and Sec-ond Sam-uel, Two Kings, Two Chron-i-cl-es, Ez-ra, Neh-e-mi-ah, Esth-'er, Job.

Psalms, Prov-erbs, E-ccles-i-as-tes, Song of Sol-o-mon, I-sa-iah, Jer-e-mi-ah, Lam-en-

ta-tions, E-zek-i-el, Dan-iel, Ho-se-a, Joel, A-mos, O-bed-i-ah, Jon-ah, Mi-cah, Na-hum, Hab-ak-kuk,

Zeph-an-i-ah, Hag-ga-i, Zech-a-ri-ah, Mal-a-chi.

Shining Star Publications, Copyright © 1988, A division of Good Apple, Inc.

SS847

NEW TESTAMENT BOOKS
by Beulahmae Marchbanks

Matthew, Mark and Luke and John, The Acts and E-pist-le to the Rom-ans, First and Sec-ond Cor-in-thi-ans, Gal-a-tions, E-phe-sians, Phil-ip-pi-ans and Col-os-sians, First and Sec-ond Thess-a-lon-i-ans, First and Sec-ond Tim-o-thy, Ti-tus, Phi-le-mon, Heb-rews and James... First, Sec-ond Pet-er, First, Sec-ond, Third John, and Jude and Rev-e-la-tion...

DOWN THE BIBLE PATH

The Bible was not written in a short time. It took hundreds of years and God used many people to complete it. It is one Book made up of many books, like one path made of many stones. Follow the path below through the Bible and become more familiar with God's Word.

START → GENESIS → EXODUS → LEVITICUS → NUMBERS → DEUTERONOMY → Name five books of Law, or return to Genesis. → JOSHUA → JUDGES

AMOS → OBADIAH → JONAH → MICAH (left column going down); top row: JOEL → HOSEA → Name five major prophets, or return to Isaiah. → DANIEL → EZEKIEL → LAMENTATIONS → JEREMIAH → ISAIAH

NAHUM → HABAKKUK → ZEPHANIAH → HAGGAI → ZECHARIAH → MALACHI

Name one New Testament book of prophecy. → REVELATION → Name one New Testament writer. → JUDE → III JOHN → II JOHN → I JOHN → II PETER → I PETER → JAMES → HEBREWS → PHILEMON

FINISH

DIRECTIONS:
1. Duplicate gameboard and mount on poster board.
2. Use different color buttons as markers.
3. Attach a cardboard spinner to wheel with a paper fastener.
4. Advance by the number you spin.

Spinner: 1, 2, 3, 4

Board spaces:
RUTH | I SAMUEL | II SAMUEL | I KINGS | II KINGS | I CHRONICLES | II CHRONICLES | EZRA | NEHEMIAH | ESTHER | What two Old Testament history books are named after women? Return to Joshua if you cannot answer.

Name five books of poetry, or return to Job. | SONG OF SOLOMON | ECCLESIASTES | PROVERBS | PSALMS | JOB

What minor prophet tells a big fish story? Return to Hosea if you do not know. | MATTHEW | MARK | LUKE | JOHN | Return to Matthew if you cannot name four books that tell of Jesus' life. | ACTS | What book tells the history of the early church?

TITUS | II TIMOTHY | I TIMOTHY | II THESSALONIANS | I THESSALONIANS | COLOSSIANS | PHILIPPIANS | EPHESIANS | GALATIANS | II CORINTHIANS | I CORINTHIANS | ROMANS

Shining Star Publications, Copyright © 1988, A division of Good Apple, Inc.

GENESIS	**EXODUS**
LEVITICUS	**NUMBERS**
DEUTERONOMY	**JOSHUA**
JUDGES	**RUTH**
I SAMUEL	**II SAMUEL**
I KINGS	**II KINGS**

O.T. LAW 2	O.T. LAW 1
0 BIBLE 2	0 BIBLE 1
O.T. LAW 4	O.T. LAW 3
0 BIBLE 4	0 BIBLE 3
O.T. HISTORY 1	O.T. LAW 5
0 BIBLE 6	0 BIBLE 5
O.T. HISTORY 3	O.T. HISTORY 2
0 BIBLE 8	0 BIBLE 7
O.T. HISTORY 5	O.T. HISTORY 4
0 BIBLE 10	0 BIBLE 9
O.T. HISTORY 7	O.T. HISTORY 6
0 BIBLE 12	0 BIBLE 11

Shining Star Publications, Copyright © 1988, A division of Good Apple, Inc.   SS847

I CHRONICLES	II CHRONICLES
EZRA	NEHEMIAH
ESTHER	JOB
PSALMS	PROVERBS
ECCLESIASTES	SONG OF SOLOMON
ISAIAH	JEREMIAH

O.T. HISTORY 9 0 BIBLE 14	O.T. HISTORY 8 0 BIBLE 13
O.T. HISTORY 11 0 BIBLE 16	O.T. HISTORY 10 0 BIBLE 15
O.T. POETRY 1 0 BIBLE 18	O.T. HISTORY 12 0 BIBLE 17
O.T. POETRY 3 0 BIBLE 20	O.T. POETRY 2 0 BIBLE 19
O.T. POETRY 5 0 BIBLE 22	O.T. POETRY 4 0 BIBLE 21
O.T. PROPHECY 2 0 BIBLE 24	O.T. PROPHECY 1 0 BIBLE 23

Shining Star Publications, Copyright © 1988, A division of Good Apple, Inc.

LAMENTATIONS	EZEKIEL
DANIEL	HOSEA
JOEL	AMOS
OBADIAH	JONAH
MICAH	NAHUM
HABAKKUK	ZEPHANIAH

O.T. PROPHECY 4	O.T. PROPHECY 3
0 BIBLE 26	0 BIBLE 25
O.T. PROPHECY 6	O.T. PROPHECY 5
0 BIBLE 28	0 BIBLE 27
O.T. PROPHECY 8	O.T. PROPHECY 7
0 BIBLE 30	0 BIBLE 29
O.T. PROPHECY 10	O.T. PROPHECY 9
0 BIBLE 32	0 BIBLE 31
O.T. PROPHECY 12	O.T. PROPHECY 11
0 BIBLE 34	0 BIBLE 33
O.T. PROPHECY 14	O.T. PROPHECY 13
0 BIBLE 36	0 BIBLE 35

HAGGAI	ZECHARIAH
MALACHI	MATTHEW
MARK	LUKE
JOHN	ACTS
ROMANS	I CORINTHIANS
II CORINTHIANS	GALATIANS

O.T. PROPHECY 16	O.T. PROPHECY 15
0 BIBLE 38	0 BIBLE 37
N.T. GOSPELS 1	O.T. PROPHECY 17
0 BIBLE 40	0 BIBLE 39
N.T. GOSPELS 3	N.T. GOSPELS 2
0 BIBLE 42	0 BIBLE 41
N.T. HISTORY 4	N.T. GOSPELS 4
0 BIBLE 44	0 BIBLE 43
N.T. LETTERS 2	N.T. LETTERS 1
0 BIBLE 46	0 BIBLE 45
N.T. LETTERS 4	N.T. LETTERS 3
0 BIBLE 48	0 BIBLE 47

EPHESIANS	PHILIPPIANS
COLOSSIANS	I THESSALONIANS
II THESSALONIANS	I TIMOTHY
II TIMOTHY	TITUS
PHILEMON	HEBREWS
JAMES	I PETER

N.T. LETTERS 6	N.T. LETTERS 5
0 BIBLE 50	0 BIBLE 49
N.T. LETTERS 8	N.T. LETTERS 7
0 BIBLE 52	0 BIBLE 51
N.T. LETTERS 10	N.T. LETTERS 9
0 BIBLE 54	0 BIBLE 53
N.T. LETTERS 12	N.T. LETTERS 11
0 BIBLE 56	0 BIBLE 55
N.T. LETTERS 14	N.T. LETTERS 13
0 BIBLE 58	0 BIBLE 57
N.T. LETTERS 16	N.T. LETTERS 15
0 BIBLE 60	0 BIBLE 59

II PETER	I JOHN
II JOHN	III JOHN
JUDE	REVELATION

GAMES CONT'D.

2. Mix up the cards. Divide them into two equal numbers of thirty-three. Divide the children into two equal groups. Lay the cards facedown on two tables. With an adult supervising each table, let the children take turns guessing books from the information on the back. The adult can check without revealing the card. If the guess was correct, the card can be turned faceup. If it was incorrect, the card can be returned to its facedown position. The first group to get all of their cards in the faceup position wins.

FINDING BOOKS IN THE BIBLE:

1. Make sure each child has a Bible (preferably his own). Divide the children into two teams. At random, hold a card up. The first child to find the first chapter of that book in his Bible, scores for his team. The cards can be placed in separate piles and counted at the end to determine the winner.

2. At random, give out at least three cards to each child. On the command of "go," see who can first locate the first chapter of each of three books named on his cards.

N.T. LETTERS 18	N.T. LETTERS 17
0 BIBLE 62	0 BIBLE 61
N.T. LETTERS 20	N.T. LETTERS 19
0 BIBLE 64	0 BIBLE 63
N.T. PROPHECY 1	N.T. LETTERS 21
0 BIBLE 66	0 BIBLE 65

ACTIVE GAME:

1. Find a category which matches the number of children you have, or play more than once using smaller categories, until every child has had a chance to play at least once. Give each child a card which he is not to look at until the command is given. Tell them that on the command of "go," they are to arrange themselves in order of the books in that category.

2. Hide the cards of a category (or the entire Bible) around the room. Let the children look for the cards and arrange them in the proper sequence as they find them.

3. Using masking tape and construction paper, make two "Bible Bingo" cards on your classroom floor. (Room not big enough? Use an area of the fellowship hall or parking lot.) Let your students be the markers. Draw the cards at random. The group that gets a straight line first wins.

ANSWER KEY

FUN TO DO page 9
DOWN
1. Woman
3. Sun
4. Trees

ACROSS
2. Man
3. Star

WHAT ABOUT MOSES? page 24
GROUP 1
1. Egypt
2. Found and adopted by Pharoah's daughter.
3. He killed an Egyptian.

GROUP 2
1. Midian
2. Zipporah
3. Jethro
4. Kept the flocks
5. God spoke to him through a burning bush and ordered him to go back to Egypt to bring Israelites out.
6. Himself
7. Yes, finally

GROUP 3
1. Ten Commandments
2. No
3. 120

PICTURE SEQUENCING page 34
4 2
1 5
6 3

HOW MANY? page 37
Flour 30 measures
Fat oxen 1   0
Meal 60 measures (threescore)
Sheep 100
Oxen out of pasture 20
Harts
Roebucks
Fallowdeer
Fowl

THE TOOLS OF DAVID page 39
harp, crook, sling, stones, crown, sword

THE SOURCE OF WISDOM page 55
Proverbs 1:5 hear, learning
Proverbs 2:6 giveth, mouth, knowledge, understanding
Proverbs 3:35 inherit, glory, shame
Proverbs 8:11 rubies
Proverbs 9:10 beginning of wisdom, holy

WISDOM TREASURE HUNT page 64
GRADE 1
1. Door
2. Fruit
3. Window
4. Dog

GRADE 2
1. Fruit
2. Bed
3. Door
4. Dog

THE STORY OF JONAH page 67
GROUP 1
1. Go to Nineveh and preach
2. Caught a ship for Tarshish
3. Storm
4. Throw him overboard
5. No
6. Yes
7. Great fish swallowed him

GROUP 2
1. Prayed
2. To pay what he vowed
3. The fish vomited Jonah out on dry land.

GROUP 3
1. Go to Nineveh
2. He went.
3. Yes
4. Fasted and mourned
5. Decided not to destroy Nineveh

GROUP 4
1. No
2. Vine
3. Yes

PUZZLE PAGE page 73
DOWN
1. Fish
2. Jonah

ACROSS
3. Obey
4. Listen
5. Ship

OTHER BIBLE PEOPLE WHO DID NOT LISTEN page 74
MOSES
1. Speak to the rock
2. Hit the rock with his rod
3. God did not tell him to hit the rock with the rod.
4. Moses and Aaron did not get to enter promised land

SAMSON
1. Cut
2. He told Delilah.
3. He lost his strength.

RICH YOUNG RULER
1. How to inherit eternal life
2. Keep commandments, sell all and give to poor
3. No
4. Sorrowful

PETER
1. Deny Him
2. No
3. Yes

WHO WAS THIS MAN JOHN? page 78
1. Zacharias
2. Priest
3. Elisabeth
4. Old
5. None
6. An angel of the Lord
7. He and Elisabeth would be given a son.
8. Wine or strong drink
9. He told him he wouldn't be able to speak.)
10. Zacharias
11. After naming his son John
12. Be called the prophet of the Highest
13. Grew and was strong in spirit

THE ORDER OF JOHN'S LIFE page 87
A-3 B-4
C-5 D-1
E-2 F-6

PUZZLE PAGE page 117

```
X F A R M E R T V M A C
Z I N N K E E P E R R M
I S W E R T Y U I R V B
P H Y S I C I A N C O P
U E S D F G H J K H K L
W R Z X C V B N M A B C
U M T R E W Q P U N L S
T A X C O L L E C T O R
V N M N S H E P H E R D
L E V M S O E C K H Y T
```

HOW MANY WORDS?

fish, her, man, an, is, she, he

Shining Star Publications, Copyright © 1988, A division of Good Apple, Inc.   SS847

AWARD CERTIFICATES

BIBLE KNOWLEDGE AWARD

This award is presented to

_____

for learning

_____

Name _____

Date _____

SUPER STAR

This award is presented to

_____

for memorizing the books of the Old Testament.

Name _____

Date _____

GOOD MEMORY AWARD

This award is presented to

_____

for memorizing the books of the New Testament.

Name _____

Date _____